CAPITAL

CLASSICS

*Recipes
from the Junior League
of Washington*

THOMASSON·GRANT

Published by THOMASSON-GRANT, INC., Charlottesville, Virginia
Frank L. Thomasson III and John F. Grant, Directors
Project coordinated by C. Douglas Elliott and Carolyn M. Clark
Designed by BOGART-SZABO INC.

———

Studio Photography by RENEE COMET

Cover and pages 2–3, 4–5, 8–9, 28–29,
42–43, 56–57, 74–75, 98–99, 116–117, 118, 125, and 128–129
copyright © 1989 by Renée Comet.

Food styling by Lisa Cherkasky   Art directed by Rob Szabo
Support by Arlene Soodak and Marty Block

———

Additional photography copyright © 1989:

PING AMRANAND: Pages 44 (Uniphoto) and 100.
JOHN F. GRANT: Page 76. HICKEY-ROBERTSON/Southern Accents: Page 6.
ROBERT LLEWELLYN: Pages 65 and 130.
MAXWELL MACKENZIE: Pages 1, 58, and 87.
FRED J. MAROON: Pages 10, 21, 30, 37, 107, and 141.
MARTIN ROGERS: Page 51 (Uniphoto).

———

Printed in the United States of America by Progress Printing Co., Lynchburg, Virginia
Typeset by BG Composition, Baltimore, Maryland

96 95 94 93 92 91 90 89   5 4 3 2 1

Library of Congress Cataloging-in-Publication Data

Capital classics : recipes from the Junior League of Washington.
    p.   cm.
Includes index.
ISBN 0-934738-60-2
1. Cookery.   I. Junior League of Washington (Washington, D.C.)
TX714.C37   1989
641.5—dc20   89-5079
                                                   CIP

Any inquiries should be directed to the
JUNIOR LEAGUE OF WASHINGTON
3039 M Street NW   Washington DC 20007   202-337-2001

(Page 1) Grand Salon, Residence of the Belgian Ambassador

TABLE OF CONTENTS

THE JUNIOR LEAGUE OF WASHINGTON celebrates the rich traditions of entertaining in our nation's Capital. Washington D.C. is a truly international city, where classical elements blend with modern ideas, where regional and foreign cultures sparkle together and where an evening at the White House, an embassy or a neighbor's home means wonderful food graciously presented. *Capital Classics* captures the essence of Washington hospitality through its array of delicious recipes and through sumptuous photographs that display the culinary talents of Washington hostesses and provide a dynamic view of the rich historical and architectural heritage of our Capital city. The Junior League of Washington offers a series of menus as varied as a Sunday brunch with friends, an elegant luncheon, a family supper or a romantic midnight dinner. *Capital Classics* shares the style and wit of Washington and its love of good food and of beautiful entertaining.

APPETIZERS

Smoked Salmon Spread

PEARLS OF RED CAVIAR ADD A
FLAVORFUL SURPRISE

Yields 2 cups

8 ounces cream cheese, softened
¼ cup heavy cream
1 scallion, thinly sliced
1 teaspoon lemon juice
 Dash of Tabasco
4 ounces smoked salmon, shredded
3 tablespoons red salmon caviar

Combine cream cheese and heavy cream. Stir in scallion, lemon juice and Tabasco. Gently fold in salmon and 2 tablespoons caviar. Do not overmix.

❧ Spoon into serving dish and garnish with remaining 1 tablespoon caviar. Serve with water crackers or thinly sliced black bread.

Spiked Chicken Liver Pâté

SMOOTH AND SLIGHTLY INTOXICATING

Serves 18–20

1 pound chicken livers
1 cup butter
1 pound liverwurst
½ cup heavy cream
½ cup port
¼ cup brandy
½ teaspoon nutmeg
¼ teaspoon cardamom

Sauté chicken livers in butter until lightly browned. Transfer mixture to food processor. Add remaining ingredients and purée. Spoon into crocks and refrigerate for at least 1 day.

❧ This pâté makes a large quantity and freezes well.

Hot Crab Spread

SHERRY ENHANCES THIS
CREAMY APPETIZER

Serves 6–8

1   pound crab meat
16   ounces cream cheese, softened
1   tablespoon Worcestershire sauce
2   small onions, finely chopped
2   tablespoons sherry
½   cup sliced almonds

Combine all ingredients except almonds. Place in shallow casserole and top with almonds. Bake at 350 degrees until bubbly, approximately 20 to 25 minutes. Serve with assorted crackers.

Fresh Salmon Ball

HORSERADISH GIVES THIS A
SATISFYING BITE

Serves 8–10

1   pound fresh salmon fillet
8   ounces cream cheese, softened
2   tablespoons lemon juice
2   tablespoons grated onion
1   tablespoon horseradish
¾   teaspoon salt
    Worcestershire sauce to taste
    Cayenne pepper to taste
    Minced fresh parsley for garnish
¾   cup chopped pecans

Place salmon in vegetable steamer and steam for 10 minutes. Cool. Flake, being careful to remove skin and bones.

❧ Combine salmon with cream cheese, lemon juice, onion, horseradish, salt, Worcestershire sauce and cayenne pepper. Refrigerate in bowl for 1 hour.

❧ Combine minced parsley with pecans. Shape salmon mixture into ball and cover with parsley and pecans.

Capital Cheese

STORE IN CROCKS OR FREEZE
UNTIL NEEDED

Yields 4–5 cups

16   ounces cream cheese
8   ounces cheddar cheese, grated
4   ounces bleu cheese
½   cup sour cream
1   tablespoon chopped chives
1   teaspoon dry mustard
2   tablespoons brandy
1   8-ounce bottle clam juice

Soften cheeses. Mix together all ingredients in blender or food processor until smooth. Chill. Serve with assorted crackers.

Bleu Cheese Mousse

AN UNEXPECTEDLY
LIGHT TEXTURE

Serves 15–20

6   eggs, separated
6   tablespoons plus 1½ cups heavy cream
1½ tablespoons unflavored gelatin
4   tablespoons cold water
¾   pound bleu cheese
    Watercress for garnish

In saucepan over low heat, beat egg yolks with 6 tablespoons heavy cream until smooth. Remove from heat.

❧ Combine gelatin with cold water. Place bowl in hot water until gelatin dissolves. Add gelatin to egg yolk mixture.

❧ Press bleu cheese through sieve and add to above mixture. Cool thoroughly.

❧ Whip remaining 1½ cups heavy cream and fold into egg mixture. Beat 3 egg whites until stiff. Fold into cream and egg mixture.

❧ Pour mousse into oiled mold and chill for at least 2 hours. Unmold onto platter and garnish with watercress. Serve with toast rounds or crackers.

Herbed Chicken Liver Pâté

AN ARRAY OF SEASONINGS ENHANCES
THIS PATE

Serves 12

1   stalk celery, coarsely chopped
2   sprigs parsley
6   peppercorns
1   pound chicken livers
1   teaspoon salt
½   teaspoon Tabasco
1   cup butter, softened
½   teaspoon nutmeg
2   teaspoons dry mustard
¼   teaspoon ground cloves
5   tablespoons minced onion
1   clove garlic, minced
2   generous tablespoons cognac
2   hard-boiled eggs, chopped

Boil celery, parsley and peppercorns in 1 quart water for 5 minutes. Add chicken livers. Cover and simmer 10 minutes. Drain.

❧ Transfer chicken livers to blender or food processor. Add salt, Tabasco, butter, nutmeg, dry mustard, cloves, onion, garlic and cognac. Process until smooth.

❧ Serve garnished with eggs. This pâté can be chilled but does not freeze well.

Smoked Trout Pâté

SUBSTITUTE SMOKED MACKEREL
FOR A CHANGE

Serves 8–10

8   ounces cream cheese, softened
¼   cup mayonnaise
1   tablespoon horseradish
    Juice of 1 lemon
    Chopped fresh dill to taste
1   smoked trout, boned and flaked

Blend cream cheese, mayonnaise, horseradish and lemon juice until smooth. Stir in dill and trout. Chill.

❧ Serve with dark bread or bagel chips.

Creamy Shrimp Dip

BEST WITH CRISP CUT VEGETABLES
OR RYE CRACKERS

Yields 2½ cups

1   **cup mayonnaise**
½   **cup sour cream**
2   **tablespoons catsup**
2   **tablespoons minced onion**
2   **tablespoons dry sherry**
¼   **teaspoon cayenne pepper**
1   **teaspoon Worcestershire sauce**
1   **pound shrimp, cooked, peeled and chopped**

Blend mayonnaise, sour cream, catsup, onion, sherry, cayenne pepper and Worcestershire sauce. Add shrimp and mix well. Refrigerate up to 5 hours before serving.

Black Bean Pâté with Spring Onion Sauce

FROM CHEF ALISON G. SWOPE,
NEW HEIGHTS RESTAURANT

Serves 16–18

4   **cups dried black beans**
1   **large onion, chopped**
6   **cloves garlic, minced**
1   **3″ piece of ginger, chopped**
3   **tablespoons butter or oil**
1   **cup sour cream**
6   **eggs**
2   **teaspoons salt**
1   **tablespoon pepper**
1   **red bell pepper, cut into thin strips**
16   **ounces feta cheese, cubed**

Cook beans in rapidly boiling water until soft, approximately 45 minutes. Drain and let cool.

❦ Sauté onion, garlic and ginger in butter until soft and transparent. Set aside to cool.

❦ Transfer black beans to food processor and pulse briefly until beans are coarsely chopped. Place beans in large bowl with onion mixture. Add sour cream, eggs, salt and pepper. Mix until combined.

❦ Place mixture in buttered loaf pan or turéen. Cover with buttered foil. Place loaf pan in larger baking pan and fill with enough hot water to come halfway up the sides of loaf pan.

❦ Bake at 350 degrees approximately 1 hour and 20 minutes, or until firm.

❦ Cool completely. Slice ¼″ to ½″ thick.

❦ To serve, fan 2 slices of pâté on plate. Top with spring onion sauce. Garnish with red pepper slices and about 1 ounce of feta cheese.

Spring Onion Sauce:
1   **egg yolk**
½   **cup red wine vinegar**
2   **tablespoons Dijon mustard**
2   **spring onions with tops**
3   **cloves garlic**
1   **teaspoon sugar**
1½   **cups olive oil**
     Salt and pepper to taste

In food processor, combine egg yolk, vinegar, mustard, onions, garlic and sugar. Process until well blended.

❦ With machine running, add olive oil in a slow, steady stream through feeder tube. Season with salt and pepper.

Tangy Radish Dip

SERVE IN A HOLLOWED-OUT CABBAGE

Yields 1½ cups

1 cup finely chopped radishes
8 ounces cream cheese
1 garlic clove, minced
1 tablespoon lemon juice
¾ teaspoon salt
½ teaspoon dill
Pepper to taste

Combine all ingredients and mix well. Chill at least 4 hours. Serve with raw vegetables.

Corned Beef in Rye

PERFECT FOR INFORMAL GATHERINGS

Serves 10–12

1⅓ cups sour cream
1⅓ cups mayonnaise
2 teaspoons dill seed
2 tablespoons dried onion flakes
10 ounces pressed corned beef, shredded
2 tablespoons chopped parsley
1 round loaf dark rye, pumpernickel or multi-grain bread

Mix first 6 ingredients until well blended. Refrigerate at least 1 hour.

🍴 Hollow out bread, cutting removed bread into bite-sized pieces. Just before serving, place corned beef mixture in bread. Serve with the bite-sized pieces of bread.

Spicy Salsa

FOR THAT HOMEMADE TOUCH

Yields 2 cups

1 14½-ounce can stewed tomatoes, undrained
6 scallions, chopped
1 4-ounce can chopped green chilies, undrained
1 bottled jalapeño pepper, seeded and minced

Chop tomatoes. Mix tomatoes and juice with other ingredients. Refrigerate for several hours. Serve with tortilla chips.

Cheddar Pecan Toasts

PERFECT WITH A BOWL OF SOUP

Yields 48 squares

½ cup chopped pecans
1 cup grated sharp cheddar cheese
1 teaspoon grated onion
½ cup mayonnaise
8 slices bacon, cooked and crumbled
12 slices melba-thin bread, whole wheat or white

Combine pecans, cheese, onion, mayonnaise and bacon. Trim crusts and spread bread with cheese mixture. Cut each slice into 4 squares. Bake at 350 degrees for 10 to 15 minutes.

Cheese Puffs

STORE IN FREEZER FOR UNEXPECTED GUESTS

Serves 6–8

1 cup butter
8 ounces cream cheese, cubed
8 ounces sharp cheddar cheese, grated
½ teaspoon cayenne pepper
2 cloves garlic, crushed (optional)
2 egg whites
   Large loaf Italian bread

Melt butter, cream cheese and cheddar cheese in top of double boiler. Stir in pepper and garlic until blended.

❧ Beat egg whites until stiff and fold into cheese mixture. Keep mixture warm.

❧ Cube bread, leaving crust on, and dip into mixture. Place on cookie sheet and freeze, then store in plastic bags until needed. Bake frozen cheese puffs at 400 degrees for 10 minutes.

Parmesan Puffs

SERVE WITH A GOOD RED WINE

Yields 24 appetizers

6 slices melba-thin whole wheat bread
½ cup mayonnaise
⅓ cup grated Parmesan cheese
2 tablespoons grated onion

Cut 4 small circles from each slice of bread. Bake the bread rounds at 350 degrees until lightly toasted, approximately 5 minutes.

❧ Combine mayonnaise, Parmesan and onion. Pipe mixture onto toast rounds. Rounds can be frozen at this point.

❧ Bake rounds at 375 degrees for 10 minutes or until topping is lightly browned.

Cheese-Stuffed Mushrooms

PERFECT WITH COCKTAILS

Serves 8–10

8 ounces cream cheese, softened
½ cup Parmesan cheese
1 clove garlic, crushed
   Dash of Tabasco
1 pound fresh mushrooms, stems removed

B lend cream cheese, Parmesan cheese, garlic and Tabasco. Stuff mushrooms with mixture and place in baking dish. Cover and refrigerate several hours.

❦ Bake at 350 degrees for 10 minutes, then broil just until cheese is lightly browned.

Neapolitan Mushrooms

USE HOT OR SWEET SAUSAGE FOR THIS
SATISFYING APPETIZER

Serves 10–15

½ pound Italian sausage, casings removed
30 large mushrooms, stems removed
¼ cup olive oil
1 cup seasoned Italian bread crumbs
4 ounces tomato paste
2 cloves garlic, crushed
2 ounces grated Parmesan cheese, plus extra for topping

I n skillet, cook sausage until lightly browned. Drain and set aside.

❦ Rub mushroom caps with olive oil. Combine sausage, bread crumbs, tomato paste, garlic and cheese. Mix well. Fill mushroom caps with mixture.

❦ Coat shallow baking dish with olive oil. Place mushrooms in dish. Sprinkle with additional cheese and any remaining oil. Bake at 375 degrees for 15 to 20 minutes until mushrooms are just tender.

Sesame Asparagus Canapés

SESAME SEEDS UPDATE THIS CLASSIC

Yields 36

12 slices melba-thin white bread
5 ounces Boursin cheese
1 can asparagus spears
½ cup butter, melted
¼ cup Parmesan cheese
¾ cup sesame seeds

R emove crusts from bread and flatten with rolling pin. Spread each slice with Boursin cheese. Place asparagus spear on top of each and roll up.

❦ Cut above into thirds. Dip in melted butter. Roll in mixture of Parmesan cheese and sesame seeds.

❦ Bake at 425 degrees for 10 to 12 minutes.

Supreme Artichoke Squares

A FAVORITE BLEND OF CHEESE AND
ARTICHOKES

Serves 6–8

2 6-ounce jars marinated artichoke hearts
1 small onion, finely chopped
1 clove garlic, crushed
4 eggs, slightly beaten
¼ cup dried bread crumbs
¼ teaspoon salt
¼ teaspoon pepper
¼ teaspoon oregano
¼ teaspoon Tabasco
½ pound sharp cheddar cheese, grated
2 tablespoons chopped fresh parsley

Drain marinade from 1 jar of artichokes into frying pan. Sauté onion and garlic in marinade.

❧ Drain other jar of artichokes, discarding marinade. Press all artichoke hearts between paper towels to remove excess liquid. Chop finely and set aside.

❧ Combine eggs, bread crumbs and seasonings. Stir in cheese, parsley, artichoke hearts, onion and garlic and mix well.

❧ Spread mixture evenly in 7″ × 11″ pan. Bake at 325 degrees for 30 minutes. Cut into squares. Serve immediately or wrap in foil and refrigerate or freeze until ready to reheat.

Spinach Balls with Mustard Sauce

THE SAUCE IS HOT AND SPICY

Yields approximately 4 dozen

2 10-ounce packages frozen chopped spinach, thawed and drained well
2 cups herbed stuffing mix
1 cup grated Parmesan cheese
¾ cup butter, melted
8 scallions, finely chopped
4 eggs, beaten
   Dash of nutmeg
   Salt and pepper to taste

Combine all ingredients and mix well. Roll into bite-sized balls and refrigerate until ready to bake, or freeze for future use.

❧ Place spinach balls on ungreased baking sheet. Bake at 350 degrees until golden brown, approximately 10 to 15 minutes.

Mustard Sauce:
Yields 1 cup

½ cup dry mustard
½ cup white vinegar
¼ cup sugar
1 egg yolk

❧ Combine mustard and vinegar. Cover and let stand at room temperature for 4 hours.

❧ Mix sugar and egg yolk in small bowl. Add mustard mixture, stirring until thickened. Cover and chill. Let mustard sauce come to room temperature before serving.

Crab Wontons

ESPECIALLY GOOD SERVED WITH OUR HOT
MUSTARD SAUCE

Yields 30–40

½ **pound fresh backfin crab meat**
6 **ounces cream cheese, softened**
½ **teaspoon white Worcestershire sauce**
1 **clove garlic, crushed**
1 **package wonton skins**
2 **egg yolks, slightly beaten**
  Vegetable oil

Combine crab meat, cream cheese, white Worcestershire sauce and garlic. Mix well. Place ¾ to 1 teaspoon of mixture on each wonton square. Fold into triangles and brush on egg yolk to seal wonton.

❧ Heat oil in deep fryer. Cook wontons, a few at a time, until brown, approximately 30 seconds. Drain on paper towels. Serve immediately.

Beggars' Pouches

EACH LITTLE POUCH HIDES A
CAVIAR SURPRISE

Serves 6–8

2 **eggs, beaten**
  Pinch of salt
½ **cup unbleached flour**
¼ **cup cake flour**
1 **cup milk**
2 **tablespoons butter, melted**
2 **tablespoons beer**
⅓ **cup clarified butter**
2 **bunches chives**
8 **ounces crème fraîche**
4 **ounces black caviar**

Blend eggs with salt and flours. Gradually add milk, blending thoroughly. Mix in melted butter and beer. Let mixture stand at room temperature for 30 minutes.

❧ Brush bottom of 6″ cast-iron skillet with clarified butter. (Do not use synthetic brush; it will melt.) Heat over medium-high heat until butter is hot enough to smoke.

❧ Pour just enough batter into skillet to coat bottom, quickly pouring off any excess. Use spatula to turn crepe when edges are brown. After no more than 30 seconds, remove crepe to a sheet of waxed paper. Repeat procedure until all the batter is used, placing a sheet of waxed paper between crepes. When cooled, crepes may be wrapped tightly and refrigerated or frozen until ready to use.

❧ To assemble pouches, spoon a tablespoon of crème fraîche onto wrong side of each crepe. Top each with a teaspoon of caviar.

❧ Gather up edges of each crepe to make a little pouch. Tie with chive stems which have been run under hot water to soften.

❧ Place finished pouches on a greased baking sheet. Bake at 450 degrees for 2 to 3 minutes.

Crab Tassies

THESE TARTS HAVE A RICH CRAB FILLING

Yields 24

½ cup butter, softened
3 ounces cream cheese, softened
1 cup flour
¼ teaspoon salt
1 pound crab meat
½ cup mayonnaise
1 tablespoon lemon juice
¼ cup finely chopped celery
2 small scallions, finely chopped
½ cup grated Swiss cheese
½ teaspoon Worcestershire sauce
¼ teaspoon seasoned salt
   Dash of Tabasco

Cream butter and cream cheese. Stir in flour and salt. Roll into 24 small balls and chill 1 hour. Press into tiny muffin tins, about 1¾″ in diameter.

❦ Mix crab with remaining ingredients. Spoon into unbaked shells and bake at 350 degrees until golden, approximately 30 minutes.

Stone Crab Claws with Four Pepper Sauce

TRY THIS SAUCE WITH OTHER TYPES OF SEAFOOD

Serves 4

1 red pepper
1 yellow pepper
1 green chili pepper
2 jalapeño peppers
¼ cup wine vinegar
⅓ cup olive oil
½ cup chopped cilantro
½ cup chopped parsley
   Salt and pepper to taste
12–16 stone crab claws

Seed and finely chop the 5 peppers. Combine all ingredients except crab in bowl and refrigerate for at least 2 hours.

❦ Serve with chilled crab claws.

Shrimp Vinaigrette

A SIMPLE AND SUMPTUOUS OFFERING

Serves 4–6

1 pound shrimp, cooked, peeled and deveined
⅓ cup thinly sliced onions
2 teaspoons sugar
2 teaspoons salt
2 tablespoons Worcestershire sauce
¼ cup catsup
½ cup cider vinegar
½ cup vegetable oil
   Cayenne pepper to taste
½ teaspoon dry mustard
   Watercress for garnish

In glass dish, layer shrimp and onions. Blend remaining ingredients and pour over shrimp. Cover and refrigerate for several hours or overnight.

❦ Drain shrimp and arrange on plate. Garnish with watercress.

Cheese Straws

Yields 6 dozen

1 **pound Old English cheese, grated**
1 **cup butter, softened**
3 **cups sifted flour**
½ **teaspoon salt**
   Cayenne pepper to taste

Bring grated cheese to room temperature. Beat cheese and butter until fluffy. Add flour half a cup at a time until well blended. Add salt and cayenne pepper.

❦ Place mixture in pastry bag fitted with star tip. On greased cookie sheet, pipe strips the full length of sheet.

❦ Bake at 350 degrees until golden, but not brown, approximately 10 to 12 minutes. Remove at once onto waxed paper and break into desired lengths.

Dumbarton Oaks

COCKTAILS

CRAB TASSIES
BEGGARS' POUCHES
TANGY RADISH DIP WITH VEGETABLES
SMOKED TROUT PATE
SPINACH-STUFFED CHERRY TOMATOES

Spinach-Stuffed Cherry Tomatoes

A COLORFUL APPETIZER OR SIDE DISH

Yields 36

36 cherry tomatoes
1 8-ounce package frozen chopped spinach, thawed
½ cup mayonnaise
½ cup sour cream
1 teaspoon dried buttermilk ranch dressing mix
3 scallions, chopped
6–8 slices bacon, cooked and crumbled

Remove tops from tomatoes and scoop out pulp. Turn tomatoes upside down on a paper towel to drain.

❦ Squeeze liquid from spinach and mix with remaining ingredients, blending well. Stuff tomatoes with mixture.

Baked Shrimp and Cheese

A DIVINE FIRST COURSE

Serves 6

½ cup butter
1 onion, chopped
2 cloves garlic, minced
4 bay leaves
2 tablespoons flour
1 cup light cream
1 teaspoon curry powder
⅓ cup dry white wine
1 pound shrimp, cooked and shelled
½ pound Swiss cheese, grated

Sauté onion, garlic and bay leaves in butter until onions are lightly browned. Remove bay leaves and strain butter into saucepan, reserving onion mixture.

❦ Add flour to butter and cook over low heat until bubbly. Slowly stir in cream and cook until sauce is medium thick. Add curry and wine and stir until smooth. Stir in onion mixture.

❦ Divide shrimp among 6 buttered ramekins or baking shells. Cover with sauce and sprinkle with cheese. Bake at 350 degrees until cheese is melted, approximately 5 minutes. Broil until cheese is lightly browned.

Marinated Chicken Wings

SWEET AND SPICY NIBBLES

Serves 10–12

1 cup dark brown sugar
1 cup soy sauce
3 teaspoons ginger
3 teaspoons dry mustard
2 teaspoons minced garlic
5 pounds chicken wings

Combine first 5 ingredients. Mix well. Pour over chicken. Marinate overnight.

❦ Drain marinade and reserve. Bake at 350 degrees for 45 minutes, basting occasionally with reserved marinade.

Sweet Chili Shrimp

Serves 6–8

½ cup mayonnaise
½ cup chili sauce
2 tablespoons sweet pickle relish
1 teaspoon minced green pepper
2 hard-boiled eggs, finely chopped
1 teaspoon prepared mustard
2 pounds shrimp, cooked, peeled and deveined
  Bibb lettuce

Combine mayonnaise, chili sauce, pickle relish, green pepper, eggs and mustard. Refrigerate overnight.

❧ Several hours before serving, combine sauce with shrimp and refrigerate until serving time. Serve on individual plates lined with Bibb lettuce.

Lobster Benedict Appetizer

FROM RIDGEWELL'S CATERERS

Yields 20

4 2-ounce lobster tails
10 asparagus tips
4 tablespoons unsalted butter
20 raw quail eggs
20 slices French bread, cut ¼" thick

Orange Hollandaise:
1 blood orange
2 egg yolks
½ cup clarified butter
  Salt and white pepper to taste

Steam lobster tails for 6 minutes. Remove meat from shells and cool. Cut each tail into 5 slices to create medallions.

❧ Blanch asparagus tips until just tender, approximately 1½ minutes. Slice in half lengthwise and keep warm.

❧ To prepare Orange Hollandaise, grate orange peel. Squeeze the juice from orange and boil with grated peel until reduced by half. Cool. Whisk egg yolks in a double boiler over medium heat. Add orange juice and cook, stirring constantly, until sauce thickens. Pour in clarified butter in very small amounts and continue whisking. Season with salt and pepper. Keep sauce warm, as any change in temperature will cause it to separate.

❧ Sauté a few lobster slices at a time in 2 tablespoons butter, approximately 30 seconds per side. Repeat with remaining lobster medallions, adding more butter if needed.

❧ Fry quail eggs, sunny-side-up, in remaining butter, being careful not to overcook the yolk.

❧ Lightly butter French bread and broil until just brown.

❧ To assemble Lobster Benedict, place 1 slice of French bread on a small plate. Top with a lobster medallion, a quail egg and 2 asparagus halves. Garnish with Orange Hollandaise.

Carpaccio of Fresh Tuna

FOR SUSHI LOVERS

Serves 2

- 4 ounces fresh tuna or swordfish
- 2 egg yolks
- 2 teaspoons lime juice
- 1 teaspoon each fresh basil, tarragon, parsley and chives
- ½ teaspoon minced ginger
- ½ teaspoon minced garlic
- 10 capers
  Lemon slices
  Fresh herb sprigs

Oil 2 pieces of plastic wrap. Place tuna between plastic wrap and pound tuna until flat. Carefully peel off plastic wrap. Slice tuna and divide between 2 chilled plates.

❧ Whisk together egg yolks and lime juice. Stir in fresh herbs, ginger and garlic. Cover each serving of tuna with 1 tablespoon sauce.

❧ Garnish plates with capers, lemon slices and fresh herb sprigs.

Oysters Vinaigrette

LIGHTLY POACHED OYSTERS GARNISHED
WITH AN HERBED DRESSING

Serves 6

- 2–3 dozen fresh oysters, shucked with shells reserved
  Boston or Bibb lettuce

Court Bouillon:
- 2 cups white wine
- 2 cups water
- 1 small onion
  Bouquet garni
- ¼ teaspoon rock salt
- 8 peppercorns

Ravigote Sauce:
- 1 tablespoon white wine vinegar
- 1 tablespoon Dijon mustard
- 1 cup light olive oil
- 2 tablespoons capers
- 2 tablespoons minced fresh parsley
  Pinch of tarragon
  Pinch of chervil
- 2 tablespoons chopped chives
  Salt and pepper to taste

In saucepan, combine court bouillon ingredients. Heat to boiling and simmer 30 minutes. Poach oysters in court bouillon for 1 minute. Cool oysters in liquid.

❧ To prepare ravigote sauce, combine vinegar and mustard. Add oil in a gradual thin stream, whisking constantly. Add capers, parsley, tarragon, chervil, chives, salt and pepper. Mix well. Stir in 4 tablespoons court bouillon.

❧ To serve, return oysters to shells and nestle in leaves of Boston or Bibb lettuce. Drizzle with ravigote sauce.

Mushroom Tart

AN IMPRESSIVE FIRST COURSE

Serves 8

Crust:

1   **cup flour**

½   **cup unsalted butter, softened**

5   **tablespoons cold water**

     Pinch of salt

Filling:

2   **ounces dried mushrooms (shitake, porcini, morels)**

1   **cup veal or beef stock**

2   **tablespoons unsalted butter**

¼   **cup olive oil**

1   **medium red onion, finely chopped**

½   **cup chopped parsley**

1   **tablespoon tomato paste**

     Salt and pepper to taste

3   **eggs**

½   **cup grated Parmesan cheese**

To make crust, sift flour onto work surface and cut in butter. Work in butter lightly with fingertips, then between hands to incorporate completely. Return to surface and sprinkle with water and salt. Knead gently until smooth, approximately 1 to 2 minutes. Form into ball, wrap in plastic and refrigerate 1 hour. Unwrap and knead 1 to 2 minutes. Roll into 12″ round. Place on greased 9″ tart pan with removable bottom. Prick pastry with fork, line with waxed paper and weight with beans or pastry weights. Refrigerate up to 1 hour.

❧ Bake shell at 375 degrees for 40 minutes. Remove weights and continue baking until medium brown, approximately 10 minutes.

❧ To make filling, soak mushrooms in stock for 30 minutes. Melt butter and oil in saucepan and add onion and parsley. Sauté over low heat for 10 minutes.

❧ Drain mushrooms, reserving stock, making sure all sand is removed from mushrooms. Add mushrooms to butter and herb mixture. Add tomato paste and sauté for 4 to 5 minutes, stirring occasionally. Strain reserved stock and add to mixture. Season with salt and pepper. Cook over low heat until most of stock has evaporated and mixture is thickened, approximately 30 minutes.

❧ Transfer mixture to bowl and cool. Add eggs and Parmesan cheese and mix well. Spoon mixture into baked pastry shell and bake at 375 degrees for 20 minutes. Remove from oven and cool 15 minutes before serving.

Scallops with Pernod and Leeks

LIGHTLY LACED WITH LICORICE

Serves 4 as an appetizer, 2 as an entrée

2   leeks, bulbs only, sliced and separated into rings
3   tablespoons butter
2   tablespoons chopped shallots
1   pound sea or bay scallops
2   tablespoons Pernod
¼   cup white wine
¼   cup chicken stock
1   cup light cream
   Salt and pepper to taste

Sauté leek rings in 1 tablespoon butter until soft. Set aside.

Sauté shallots in remaining 2 tablespoons butter. Add scallops and sauté until opaque. Remove from pan and keep warm.

Add Pernod to frying pan. Cook briefly. Stir in white wine and chicken stock. Boil 2 to 3 minutes. Add cream and stir. Return scallops to pan. Cook briefly. Serve scallops topped with leek rings.

Sherried Mushroom Strudel

A GOLDEN PHYLLO CRUST WRAPS A RICH FILLING

Serves 16

¾   cup unsalted butter
6   cups minced mushrooms
1   teaspoon salt
¼   teaspoon curry powder
6   tablespoons sherry
4   tablespoons chopped shallots
1   cup sour cream plus extra for garnish
1   cup plus 3 tablespoons dry bread crumbs
8   sheets phyllo dough
   Chopped scallions for garnish

Melt ¼ cup butter in skillet over medium low heat. Add mushrooms, salt, curry powder, sherry and shallots. Sauté until mushrooms are wilted and liquid is evaporated, about 20 minutes. Cool. Stir in 1 cup sour cream and 3 tablespoons bread crumbs. Refrigerate mixture overnight.

Melt remaining ½ cup butter. Brush a sheet of phyllo with melted butter and sprinkle with bread crumbs. Repeat until there are 4 layers.

Spread half the mushroom mixture evenly onto phyllo, leaving a 1″ border. Roll lengthwise, jellyroll fashion. Brush completed roll with butter and sprinkle with bread crumbs. Place on lightly greased cookie sheet. Mark 8 equal slices with a sharp knife. Repeat the above process using remaining mushroom filling and phyllo.

Bake strudels at 375 degrees until lightly browned, approximately 40 minutes. Garnish with small dollop of sour cream and chopped scallions.

Spanakopita

A SAVORY GREEK PIE

Serves 16 as an appetizer, 8 as a main dish

3 packages frozen chopped spinach
4 scallions, chopped
2 tablespoons olive oil
3 eggs, slightly beaten
¼ cup chopped parsley
2 cups cottage cheese
4 ounces feta cheese, crumbled
½ cup Parmesan cheese
1 tablespoon Greek seasoning
   Salt and pepper to taste
1 cup butter, melted
1 pound frozen phyllo dough, thawed

Cook spinach according to package directions, omitting salt. Drain and squeeze dry. Cook scallions in oil until soft. Add to spinach. Combine spinach mixture with eggs, parsley, cheeses and seasonings. Mix well and set aside.

❧ Lightly butter bottom and sides of 9″ × 13″ × 2″ baking pan.

❧ Cut phyllo sheets in half crosswise. Trim to fit pan. Layer half of phyllo sheets, 1 at a time, in pan brushing each sheet lightly with melted butter. Spread spinach mixture evenly over phyllo. Top with remaining half of phyllo sheets, brushing each sheet with melted butter.

❧ Score top layer of dough into serving size pieces with the tip of a sharp knife. Bake at 350 degrees for 40 to 45 minutes or until golden brown.

Mozzarella in Phyllo Dough

FROM CHEF KENNETH C. JURAN,
THE PARK HYATT

Serves 8

8 ounces fresh buffalo mozzarella
4 ounces ricotta cheese
1 teaspoon chopped cooked garlic
1 teaspoon chopped basil
1 teaspoon chopped oregano
   Flesh of 2 tomatoes, chopped
1 teaspoon Dijon mustard
2 ounces bread crumbs
   Salt and pepper to taste
½ box phyllo dough

Sauce:

2 cups white wine
4 stalks lemon grass
4 white peppercorns
6 shallots, chopped
2 ounces cream
1 pound butter
   Juice of 1 lemon
   Salt and pepper to taste
1 tablespoon chopped tomato flesh
1 tablespoon chopped Niçoise olives

Mix together mozzarella, ricotta, garlic, basil, oregano, tomatoes, mustard, bread crumbs, salt and pepper. Place 4 sheets phyllo dough on counter and brush with butter. Cut in half. Place approximately ¼ cup of mixture in middle of each half and pull from corners to make a small nest, enclosing mixture completely. Bake in oven at 350 degrees for 12 minutes.

❧ For sauce, reduce white wine, lemon grass, peppercorns and shallots over high heat. Add cream and reduce again. Gradually add butter, then lemon juice, salt and pepper. Add chopped tomato and olives. Place 1 spoonful of sauce on plate. Top with phyllo packet.

SOUPS

Cream of Brie Soup

MELLOW AND LUXURIOUS

Serves 6

½ cup chopped yellow onion
½ cup sliced celery
4 tablespoons butter
¼ cup flour
2 cups milk
2 cups chicken stock
¾ pound brie cheese, rind removed
   Salt and pepper to taste
   Chopped chives for garnish

In stock pot, sauté onion and celery in butter until soft and transparent. Stir in flour and cook until mixture bubbles. Remove from heat. Gradually stir in milk and chicken stock.

❧ Return to heat. Stir until soup thickens.

❧ Cube cheese. Add to stock pot and stir until melted. Season with salt and pepper. Serve immediately, garnished with chopped chives.

Light Curry Soup

SIMPLE WITH AN EXOTIC TASTE

Serves 6

4 tablespoons butter
1 large onion, sliced
2½ cups beef or chicken stock
1 teaspoon curry
¼ teaspoon ginger
¼ teaspoon nutmeg
2 tablespoons flour
1 egg
1 cup light cream
2 teaspoons dry sherry

Sauté onion in butter over low heat for 10 minutes. Allow mixture to cool slightly, then transfer to blender or food processor. Add stock, curry, ginger, nutmeg, flour and egg and purée.

❧ Return mixture to saucepan and cook over medium heat until thick. Stir in cream and sherry and heat through.

Stilton and Pear Soup

CREAM OF LEEK SOUP WITH A
SURPRISING TWIST

Serves 8

4	tablespoons butter
2	stalks celery, minced
1	large onion, minced
2	leeks, bulbs only, minced
½	cup flour
4	cups chicken stock
¼	pound Monterey Jack cheese, grated
2	cups heavy cream
¼	pound Stilton cheese, diced
3	ripe pears, peeled, cored and diced

Melt butter in large stockpot. Add celery, onions and leeks. Sauté until vegetables are soft. Sprinkle in flour and cook for 2 minutes, stirring occasionally. Gradually add 2 cups of stock, stirring constantly.

❦ Transfer mixture to food processor or blender and purée. Return to pot and add remaining stock, Monterey Jack cheese and cream. Heat through. At this point, soup may be chilled.

❦ Place Stilton and pears in individual bowls. Ladle hot or cold soup into bowls.

Chinese Black Mushroom Bisque

CHINESE MUSHROOMS ADD A RICH TOUCH

Serves 6

10–12	Chinese mushrooms
½	cup hot water
1	pound domestic mushrooms, sliced
1	tablespoon lemon juice
6	tablespoons butter
2	teaspoons minced garlic
2	tablespoons minced shallots
2	slices bread, crusts removed
4	cups chicken stock
1	cup heavy cream
¼	cup dry sherry
2	tablespoons minced parsley
	Salt and pepper to taste

Reconstitute Chinese mushrooms by soaking in ½ cup hot water for 30 minutes. Drain mushrooms, reserving liquid, and slice. Place domestic mushrooms in enough cold water to cover and add lemon juice. Let stand for 1 minute. Drain and pat dry.

❦ Melt butter in saucepan. Add garlic, shallots and mushrooms; sauté for 5 minutes. Crumble bread and add to mixture. Transfer mixture to food processor or blender and purée.

❦ Return to pan. Add chicken stock and mushroom liquid. Cook for 15 minutes. Stir in cream, sherry, parsley, salt and pepper. Heat through, but do not boil.

Madeira Mushroom Soup

A SUMPTUOUS FIRST COURSE

Serves 6

6	tablespoons butter
1	medium onion, finely chopped
1	pound mushrooms, finely chopped
3	tablespoons flour
3	cups chicken stock
1½	teaspoons salt
½	teaspoon pepper
½	cup Madeira
⅔	cup heavy cream
	Parsley for garnish

Melt butter in large saucepan. Add onion and sauté for 10 minutes or until evenly browned.

❦ Add mushrooms and cook for 2 minutes. Sprinkle in flour and cook until bubbly. Gradually stir in stock and season with salt and pepper. Bring to a boil, then cover and simmer for 10 minutes.

❦ Stir in Madeira and heavy cream. Heat through, but do not boil.

❦ Serve immediately, garnished with chopped parsley.

Chilled Pea and Lettuce Soup

AN ELEGANT SUMMER SOUP

Serves 6–8

1   10-ounce package frozen peas, partially thawed
1   medium potato, peeled and diced
1   medium onion, chopped
1   head Boston lettuce, chopped
2   cups chicken stock
1   cup heavy cream
    Juice of ½ lemon
    Salt and pepper to taste
    Mint or watercress for garnish

Combine peas, potato, onion, lettuce and 1 cup chicken stock in saucepan. Bring to a boil. Lower heat, cover and simmer for 10 minutes. Transfer to food processor or blender and purée.

❧   Return mixture to pan. Add remaining stock and simmer 5 minutes. Stir in cream and lemon juice. Season with salt and pepper. Chill for several hours.

❧   Garnish with mint or watercress.

Gingered Carrots Vichysoisse

FROM RIDGEWELL'S CATERERS

Serves 6

2   tablespoons butter
5   carrots, coarsely chopped
1   onion, coarsely chopped
8   cups chicken stock
1   potato, peeled and quartered
½" piece fresh ginger root, peeled and sliced
1   tablespoon salt
1   teaspoon ground white pepper
¾   cup heavy cream
2   tablespoons snipped chives

Melt butter in saucepan and add carrots and onion. Cook slowly for 10 minutes, stirring occasionally. Add chicken stock, potato, ginger, salt and pepper. Simmer, uncovered, for 45 minutes. Drain liquid and reserve.

❧   Purée vegetable mixture in food processor or blender and return to saucepan. Add reserved stock and bring to a boil. Reduce heat and add cream. Simmer 5 minutes. Remove from heat, cool and chill well.

❧   To serve, pour chilled soup in individual bowls and sprinkle with chives. If soup is too thick, thin with additional cream.

Chilled Curried Pea Soup

SOUP WITH A GORGEOUS CELADON HUE

Serves 6

1½ cups chicken stock
1   10-ounce package frozen peas
1   tablespoon chopped chives and additional for garnish
1   teaspoon lemon juice
1   teaspoon curry powder, or to taste
¼   teaspoon salt
¼   teaspoon pepper
½   cup half-and-half

Bring stock to a boil. Add peas and return to a boil. Cover and simmer 10 minutes.

❧   Add chives, lemon juice, curry powder, salt and pepper.

❧   Transfer to food processor or blender and purée. Chill 4 to 6 hours, or overnight.

❧   Just before serving, stir in cream and garnish with additional chives.

Cucumber Vichyssoise

A REFRESHING VERSION OF AN OLD CLASSIC

Serves 6

¼ cup chopped onion

2 cups diced, unpeeled cucumber

½ cup peeled, diced potato

2 cups chicken stock

1 teaspoon chopped parsley and additional for garnish

⅛ teaspoon pepper

¼ teaspoon dry mustard

1 cup heavy cream

Place all ingredients except cream in stockpot and bring to a boil. Cover and simmer until potatoes are just tender, approximately 10 minutes. Pour off about 1 cup stock and reserve. Transfer vegetable mixture to a blender or food processor and purée. Stir in reserved stock and correct seasoning. Chill thoroughly.

❦ When ready to serve, stir in cream and garnish with additional parsley.

Red Pepper Soup

CREATES A BEAUTIFUL FIRST COURSE

Serves 4–6

4 large red bell peppers

4 small onions, thinly sliced

6 tablespoons unsalted butter

½ potato, peeled and grated

2½ cups chicken stock

½ cup heavy cream

2 tablespoons fresh lemon juice

Salt and pepper to taste

2 tablespoons snipped fresh dill

Steam peppers until skin pulls away easily, about 25 minutes. Peel and finely chop.

❦ Melt butter in large saucepan and add peppers and onions. Cover and cook over moderately low heat, approximately 30 minutes, stirring occasionally.

❦ Add potato and chicken stock and bring to a boil. Cover and simmer over low heat, approximately 15 minutes.

❦ Transfer mixture to food processor or blender and purée in batches. Return to pan. Add cream, lemon juice, salt and pepper.

❦ Serve soup hot or chilled, garnished with fresh dill.

Cucumber Avocado Soup

A LIGHT, EASY BLENDER SOUP

Serves 4

1 cucumber, peeled, seeded and coarsely chopped

1 small ripe avocado, peeled and seeded

2 scallions, chopped

1 cup chicken stock

1 cup sour cream or yogurt

3 tablespoons lime juice

2 dashes Tabasco

Salt to taste

Blend all ingredients in food processor or blender until smooth.

❦ Chill several hours.

Charred Bell Pepper and Tomato Soup with Vermouth and Basil

FROM CHEF DOUGLAS MCNEILL,
FOUR SEASONS HOTEL.

Serves 6

2 pounds plum tomatoes
4 large red bell peppers
1 tablespoon virgin olive oil
2 cups dry vermouth
2 cups unsalted tomato juice
2 cups unsalted V-8 juice
4 tablespoons basil purée
1 teaspoon pepper
2 teaspoons salt
2 tablespoons créme fraîche
6 basil leaves for garnish

Halve tomatoes and peppers, removing stalks and seeds. Brush with olive oil. Char well on grill or in oven. (If charring on grill, apple or cherrywood chips may be added for a different flavor.) Remove skins from tomatoes and peppers and roughly chop pulp.

❧ Place tomatoes and peppers in casserole. Add vermouth and cook over low heat until reduced by half. Add tomato and V-8 juice, salt and pepper and simmer 15 minutes. Place in blender or food processor, add 3 tablespoons basil purée and purée until smooth. Pass through a fine sieve and refrigerate 3 to 4 hours or overnight.

❧ Combine 1 tablespoon créme fraîche with remaining 1 tablespoon basil purée. Refrigerate.

❧ Pour soup into chilled soup plates. Feather with créme fraîche and basil or add a dollop of créme fraîche and basil purée in the center with a basil leaf. Serve with Parslied Pistachio Anchovy Toasts.

Basil Purée:

2 bunches fresh basil
White wine

In food processor or blender, purée basil with small amount of wine.

Parslied Pistachio Anchovy Toasts:

6 tablespoons unsalted butter
3 ounces shelled pistachios
4 anchovy fillets
1 bunch Italian parsley
½ teaspoon cracked black pepper
2 tablespoons pernod
2 tablespoons chopped scallions
1 French baguette, cut into 18 slices on an angle

Place butter in food processor and cream until light and fluffy. Add all other ingredients except bread. Pulse until mixture is chopped medium fine.

❧ Spread mixture on bread slices. Bake at 350 degrees until brown. Serve warm.

Fresh Tomato Soup
with Cheese Quenelles

A REWARDING CHALLENGE FOR THE
ADVENTUROUS COOK

Serves 6

Tomato Soup:

2	slices bacon, diced
1	onion, chopped
1	small carrot, diced
1	celery heart, diced
1	clove unpeeled garlic
	Pinch of dried thyme
1	bay leaf
1	whole clove
1	sage leaf
	Pinch of fresh rosemary
½	cup tomato purée
2½	pounds fresh tomatoes, peeled, seeded and chopped
4	cups chicken stock
2	teaspoons sugar, or to taste
	Salt and white pepper to taste
	Parsley or watercress for garnish

Cheese Quenelles:

3	egg yolks
1½	tablespoons butter, melted and cooled
⅓	cup small curd cottage cheese
¼	cup white bread crumbs
¼	teaspoon freshly grated nutmeg
	Pinch of dried basil, crumbled
	Salt and white pepper to taste

Place bacon in a large skillet. Cover and cook over low heat about 5 minutes, stirring occasionally. Add onion, carrot, celery, garlic, thyme, bay leaf, clove, sage and rosemary. Cover and cook about 10 minutes or until onion is translucent, stirring occasionally. Stir in tomato purée and cook 10 minutes. Add tomatoes and stock, increase heat and bring to a boil. Reduce heat and simmer 35 minutes. Transfer soup to food processor or blender and purée. Strain and set aside.

❧ To make quenelles, mix yolks and butter in a medium bowl until smooth and frothy. Stir in remaining ingredients. Let stand at room temperature for 3 hours.

❧ Add sugar to soup and warm over low heat. Do not boil. Season soup with salt and pepper.

❧ Just before serving, bring enough water to cover quenelles to a rapid boil in a deep skillet or large saucepan. With moistened hands, form 18 small oval quenelles. Reduce water to simmer and carefully immerse quenelles. Simmer until done, about 5 minutes. Do not boil.

❧ Ladle soup into shallow bowls. Place 3 quenelles in each bowl, pointing one end of each quenelle toward the center of the bowl. Garnish with parsley or watercress.

Fresh Tomato Bisque

A WONDERFUL WAY TO USE FRESH
TOMATOES FROM YOUR GARDEN

Serves 6

2 pounds ripe tomatoes (about 6)

1 medium onion, thinly sliced

2 tablespoons butter

1 bay leaf

1 heaping tablespoon brown sugar

2 whole cloves

1 teaspoon salt

½ teaspoon pepper

2 tablespoons chopped fresh basil or
   2 teaspoons dried basil

2 cups light cream

1 cup milk

2 tablespoons chopped chives

Peel, seed and chop tomatoes. Sauté onion in butter until soft. Add tomatoes, bay leaf, brown sugar, cloves, salt, pepper and basil. Simmer, stirring occasionally, until tomatoes are thoroughly cooked, about 25 minutes.

❧ Remove and discard bay leaf and cloves. Transfer mixture to food processor or blender and purée. Blend in cream and milk. Chill several hours or overnight.

❧ Serve in chilled bowls and garnish with chives.

N Street, Georgetown

FORMAL DINNER

MADEIRA MUSHROOM SOUP

VEAL CHOPS WITH HERB MUSTARD BUTTER

TOMATOES PROVENCALE

BACON AND RADICCHIO SALAD

HAZELNUT MERINGUES WITH RASPBERRY SAUCE

Tomato Dill Soup

MAY BE SERVED HOT OR COLD

Serves 4

3 tablespoons butter

1½ cups chopped scallions, including
    green tops

2 pounds tomatoes, peeled and chopped

2 tablespoons chopped fresh dill and
   additional for garnish

2 teaspoons sugar

   Salt and pepper to taste

2 cups chicken stock

1 cup heavy cream

Sauté scallions in butter until tender. Add tomatoes, dill, sugar, salt and pepper. Cook, uncovered, until liquid is absorbed and mixture thickens.

❧ Transfer mixture to blender or food processor. Add ½ cup of chicken stock and purée mixture. Return to saucepan. Add remaining stock.

❧ Simmer 15 minutes. Add cream and heat through. Garnish with dill.

Gazpacho

4 tomatoes, peeled, seeded and finely
  chopped
2 cucumbers, peeled and chopped
5 scallions, chopped
1 green pepper, finely chopped
2½ cups tomato juice
1½ cups chicken stock
¼ cup red wine vinegar
⅓ cup olive oil
1 clove garlic, crushed
3 tablespoons chopped parsley
½ teaspoon Tabasco
  Pepper to taste
  Homemade croutons for garnish (optional)

Combine ingredients and refrigerate
several hours. Serve with croutons, if
desired.

Butternut Squash Soup

1 butternut squash
4 tablespoons butter
3 tablespoons flour
1 cup milk
2 cups chicken stock
½ teaspoon lemon juice
  Pinch of salt
⅛ teaspoon pepper
¼ teaspoon nutmeg
1 tablespoon sherry

Rub whole squash with 1 tablespoon
butter. Pierce all over with fork. Bake
at 350 degrees until tender, approximately
35 to 40 minutes. Remove from oven and
let cool.

❧ When cool to the touch, peel off stem
and skin. Remove seeds and cut squash
into chunks.

❧ Transfer mixture to food processor or
blender and purée.

❧ Melt remaining butter and stir in flour.
Slowly stir in milk. Gradually add chicken
stock, then lemon juice, seasonings and
sherry. Fold in squash and simmer gently.
If too thick, add additional milk.

Yellow Squash Soup

4 tablespoons butter
2 tablespoons vegetable oil
1 large onion, chopped
2 cloves garlic, minced
3 pounds yellow squash, thinly sliced
3 cups chicken stock
1 cup light cream
1 teaspoon salt
½ teaspoon white pepper
2 teaspoons finely chopped fresh dill and
  additional for garnish

Sauté onion and garlic in butter and oil.
Add squash and stock. Cover and cook
for 15 minutes.

❧ Transfer mixture to food processor or
blender and purée in several batches.

❧ Return to pot and add cream, salt,
pepper and dill. Heat through, stirring
constantly.

❧ Serve hot or cold, garnished with a
sprig of dill.

Iced Pineapple Mango Soup

FROM CHEF HENRY DINARDO,
WINDOWS RESTAURANT

Serves 10–12

1 large pineapple, peeled and cored
4 ripe mangoes, peeled and pitted
¼ cup mango or papaya nectar
¼ cup pineapple juice
1 tablespoon grated orange peel
¼ cup Grand Passion liqueur
4 cups heavy cream

In food processor, purée pineapple and mangoes. Add nectar, pineapple juice, orange peel and liqueur and blend. Strain mixture through fine sieve to remove fiber. Return mixture to food processor and slowly add cream. Chill for several hours before serving.

Curried Asparagus Soup

CURRY AND ASPARAGUS MAKE A
CAPTIVATING COMBINATION

Serves 6

3 tablespoons unsalted butter
3 teaspoons curry powder
1 small onion, minced
3 tablespoons flour
4 cups chicken stock
1 pound asparagus
1 small potato, peeled and diced
   Salt and pepper to taste
1 cup sour cream

Melt butter in saucepan. Add curry powder and onion and simmer until onion is soft. Blend in flour and cook 1 minute, stirring constantly. Slowly stir in chicken stock.

❧ Cut asparagus into 1″ lengths, reserving tips. Add asparagus and potato to stock and simmer until vegetables are tender, approximately 20 minutes. Add salt and pepper.

❧ Transfer the mixture to blender or food processor and purée. Return mixture to pan and stir in sour cream. Heat through. Serve garnished with reserved asparagus tips which have been cooked in boiling water until just tender.

Sherried Peach Soup

A SOPHISTICATED COLD LUNCHEON SOUP

Serves 4–6

6 large ripe peaches (or 8–10 medium peaches)
1 cup canned pineapple chunks with juice
1 cup golden sherry
¼ cup fresh lemon juice
¼ cup sugar
2 cups sour cream
   Fresh mint for garnish

Poach peaches in hot water until soft. Peel and slice.

❧ Place all ingredients except sour cream in food processor or blender and purée. Add sour cream and blend. Chill for at least 3 hours.

❧ Garnish with fresh mint.

Portuguese Soup

SERVE WITH OUR PUMPERNICKEL RYE
BREAD AND COLD BEER

Serves 10–12

2 tablespoons vegetable oil
1 clove garlic, crushed
2 cups chopped onion
4 links linguisi or hot Italian sausage
1 teaspoon salt
1 teaspoon pepper
2 15-ounce cans tomato juice
1 6-ounce can tomato paste
10 cups water
2 15-ounce cans kidney beans, drained
2 medium heads cabbage, chopped
4 large potatoes, peeled and diced
3 cups chicken stock
½ cup white vinegar

In large stockpot, sauté garlic, onion and sausage in oil for 5 minutes. Season with salt and pepper. Stir in tomato juice, tomato paste and water. Add kidney beans, cabbage, potatoes, chicken stock and vinegar. Bring to a boil. Cover and simmer for 3 hours, stirring occasionally.

Corn Chowder

BACON ADDS A SMOKEY FLAVOR

Serves 6–8

6 slices bacon
2 tablespoons butter
¾ cup chopped onion
¾ cup chopped celery
4 cups chicken stock
2 cups diced potatoes
6 cups fresh corn or 3 10-ounce packages
   frozen corn, thawed
1 cup heavy cream
   Salt and pepper to taste

Fry bacon until crisp and remove from pan. Add butter to pan and melt with bacon drippings. Add onion and celery and cook until vegetables are just tender.

❦ Pour stock into soup pot and add potatoes. Cook until tender.

❦ Purée 2 packages (4 cups) of corn in blender, adding small amount of hot stock while blending. Add blended corn, remaining whole corn, vegetables and cream to soup pot. Season with salt and pepper and heat through.

❦ Just before serving, crumble cooked bacon into soup.

Scotch Stew

A THICK, HEARTY STEW

Serves 8

1 tablespoon vegetable oil
1 pound ground lamb
1 medium onion, chopped
1 cup cooked white rice
2 cups chicken stock
2 cups beef stock
½ cup uncooked barley
1½ cups water
6–8 carrots, sliced
3–4 celery stalks, sliced
1 teaspoon lemon juice
   Pepper to taste
1 teaspoon seasoned salt
3 teaspoons minced parsley
1 teaspoon rosemary

Heat oil in iron skillet and brown lamb and onion. Drain off fat. Transfer mixture to stock pot and add remaining ingredients. Cook on low heat for at least 2 hours.

Country Beef Stew

AN EASY WINTER MEAL

Serves 8

2   pounds lean beef cubes
2   tablespoons butter
2   onions, chopped
1   48-ounce can vegetable juice
2   cups chopped celery
2½ cups chopped cabbage
2   potatoes, peeled and cubed
    Salt and pepper to taste
    Dash Tabasco (optional)

In large stock pot, brown meat on all sides in butter. Add onions and juice. Simmer 2 hours. Add celery, cabbage and potatoes and simmer an additional hour. Season to taste.

Seafood Gumbo

HEAVENLY AND HOT

Serves 6–8

½   cup butter
2   tablespoons flour
1   28-ounce can whole tomatoes
6–7 cups water
1   medium onion, chopped
1   clove garlic, crushed
1   medium green pepper, chopped
5   stalks celery, chopped
1   teaspoon ground red pepper
¼   teaspoon thyme
2   bay leaves
    Salt and pepper to taste
¼   cup uncooked rice
1   pound crab meat
3   pounds raw shrimp, peeled and deveined
2   cups sliced fresh okra

Melt butter over low heat and blend in flour, stirring continuously until brown and bubbly. Add tomatoes, water, onion, garlic, green pepper, celery, red pepper, thyme, bay leaves, salt and pepper. Simmer on low heat for 3 hours, adding additional water if necessary. Soup can be made ahead to this point and refrigerated.

❧ Add rice, crab meat, shrimp and okra and bring to a boil. Simmer for 30 minutes. Correct seasoning.

Creole Shrimp Stew

THICK AND SPICY

Serves 6

2   tablespoons vegetable oil
2   tablespoons flour
2   medium onions, chopped
2   medium cloves garlic, minced
1   28-ounce can whole tomatoes, chopped, juice included
1   16-ounce can cream-style corn
1   cup water
1   bay leaf
2   teaspoons minced parsley
    Salt, pepper and red pepper to taste
1   pound small shrimp, peeled and deveined

Heat oil in large pot and gradually stir in flour. Cook and stir over medium heat until chocolate brown in color. Add onions and garlic and cook until soft.

❧ Pour tomatoes, corn and water into pot. Add bay leaf and parsley. Season to taste.

❧ Simmer at least 1 hour, adding water if necessary to achieve desired consistency. Soup may be made ahead to this point and refrigerated. Add shrimp and simmer 15 minutes. Serve immediately.

SALADS

Summer Greek Salad

COOL, CRISP AND REFRESHING

Serves 6

3 large tomatoes, cut into wedges
1 cucumber, thinly sliced
¼ medium green pepper, cut into 1″ pieces
1 small onion, thinly sliced
8 ripe olives, pitted and quartered

Dressing:
¼ cup plus 1 tablespoon olive oil
¼ cup red wine vinegar
½ teaspoon dried whole oregano
½ teaspoon salt
¼ teaspoon pepper
⅔ cup crumbled feta cheese

Combine all salad ingredients in a salad bowl. Set aside.

❧ For dressing, combine all dressing ingredients, except cheese, in jar or blender. Pour over vegetables and toss. Chill several hours.

❧ Before serving, toss again and sprinkle with cheese.

Tabouli

WONDERFUL FOR SUMMER PICNICS

Serves 6–8

1 cup bulgur wheat
1 cup boiling water
¼ cup extra virgin olive oil
⅓ cup fresh lemon juice
1 teaspoon salt
1 large or 2 small garlic cloves, minced
½ teaspoon oregano
2 dashes cayenne pepper
½ cup chopped scallions
¾ cup finely chopped parsley
1 large tomato, diced
½ cup sliced ripe olives

Pour boiling water over bulgur and mix. Let sit for 30 minutes.

❧ In separate bowl, mix olive oil, lemon juice, salt, garlic, oregano and cayenne pepper.

❧ Add scallions, parsley, tomato and olives to bulgur. Pour oil mixture over bulgur and vegetables. Stir well. Refrigerate several hours before serving.

Broccoli Cheese Salad

A MEDLEY OF TASTES AND TEXTURES

Serves 4

1 large head broccoli, cut into florets
1 cup grated sharp cheddar cheese
1 onion, thinly sliced
½ cup mayonnaise
2 tablespoons sugar
1 tablespoon red wine vinegar
8 slices bacon, cooked crisp and crumbled

Blanch broccoli florets and cool. Toss with cheese and onion and refrigerate.

❦ Just before serving, combine mayonnaise, sugar and vinegar and toss with broccoli mixture. Sprinkle with crumbled bacon.

Endive, Watercress and Walnut Salad

THIS SALAD HAS A WONDERFUL NUTTY FLAVOR

Serves 4–6

1 dozen whole walnuts
1 teaspoon walnut oil
   Salt and pepper to taste
2 bunches watercress
2 heads endive

Vinaigrette:
1 tablespoon red wine vinegar
1 small shallot, diced
3½ tablespoons olive oil
1½ teaspoons wanut oil, or to taste
   Salt and pepper to taste

Break walnuts into large pieces and toss with oil, salt and pepper. Toast in 350 degree oven for approximately 5 minutes.

❦ Blend all vinaigrette ingredients together.

❦ Remove large stems from watercress. Cut endive leaves into thirds, removing cores. Toss greens with nuts and vinaigrette just before serving. As a variation, add crumbled bleu cheese.

Bleu Cheese Potato Salad

BLEU CHEESE ADDS AN EXTRA DIMENSION

Serves 4–6

4 large potatoes, peeled and cubed
½ cup chopped celery
½ cup sliced water chestnuts
½ cup chopped scallions
2 tablespoons minced parsley
   Salt and pepper to taste
½ teaspoon celery seed
1 cup sour cream
2–4 ounces bleu cheese, crumbled
3 tablespoons white wine vinegar

Boil potatoes until they are just tender. Drain. Combine with celery, water chestnuts, scallions, parsley, salt, pepper and celery seed.

❦ In separate bowl, combine sour cream, bleu cheese and vinegar. Pour over the potato mixture and toss. Chill overnight.

Jicama Salad

TOASTED PECANS AND JICAMA MAKE A
SPECTACULAR COMBINATION

Serves 4

2–3 bunches watercress, larger stems removed
1 large jicama, peeled and julienned
½ cup chopped, toasted pecans
½ cup Raspberry Vinaigrette

Arrange watercress on individual salad plates. Top with jicama and pecans. Drizzle with Raspberry Vinaigrette.

Raspberry Vinaigrette:
Yields 2 cups

¾ cup sugar
⅓ cup raspberry vinegar
½ teaspoon dry mustard
½ teaspoon salt
2 tablespoons minced onion
1 cup vegetable oil
4 teaspoons poppy seeds

Mix sugar, vinegar, mustard, salt and onion in blender. Slowly add oil to blender until dressing reaches a thick consistency. Stir in poppy seeds. Store dressing in tightly closed jar. (This recipe makes enough dressing for additional salads.)

Delicious —

Bacon and Radicchio Salad

HOMEMADE CROUTONS MAKE
THIS SPECIAL

Serves 6–8

1 loaf French bread, crust removed
  Oil for frying
2 cloves garlic, minced
2 tablespoons red wine vinegar
½ cup safflower oil
2 tablespoons minced fresh tarragon or
  3 tablespoons dried tarragon
1 head green leaf lettuce, torn into bite-size
  pieces
½ pound radicchio, julienned
4 slices of bacon, cooked crisp and crumbled

Cube bread. Pour 1″ of oil into a skillet and heat. Fry bread cubes in the oil until golden brown. Remove immediately and place in brown paper bag with garlic. Shake bag and set aside.

❧ Make vinaigrette by whisking together safflower oil and vinegar. Add tarragon and mix well. If using dried tarragon, steep in very hot water for 3 minutes, then drain and add to vinaigrette.

❧ Just before serving, toss vinaigrette with radicchio and green leaf lettuce. Add bacon and croutons.

Salade Rouge de Trevise Tiede aux Crevettes

FROM CHEF PIERRE CHAMBRIN,
MAISON BLANCHE

Serves 4

1½ pounds rouge de trevise (radicchio)
½ pound shrimp, peeled and deveined
1 tablespoon sherry vinegar
3 tablespoons hazelnut oil
2 tablespoons olive oil
  Salt and pepper to taste
1 tablespoon dark soy sauce
1 tablespoon Worchestershire sauce

Clean and wash radicchio. Dry between 2 towels.

❧ Cut shrimp into ½″ chunks. Combine ½ tablespoon vinegar and hazelnut oil. Mix radicchio with vinaigrette.

❧ Sauté shrimp in very hot pan with olive oil, salt and pepper. Deglaze the pan with soy sauce, Worchestershire sauce and remaining ½ tablespoon sherry vinegar. Pour on top of salad immediately. Serve at once on a warm plate.

Vegetable Medley Salad

A COLORFUL SALAD FOR
A WINTER BUFFET

Serves 6–8

- ½ cup mayonnaise
- ¼ cup sugar
- ⅓ cup tarragon
- ½ teaspoon salt
- ⅛ teaspoon pepper
- 1 head broccoli, separated into florets
- 1 head cauliflower, separated into florets
- 1 bunch fresh scallions, chopped
- 1 red pepper, chopped
- 10 pieces bacon, cooked crisp and crumbled

Combine mayonnaise, sugar, tarragon, salt and pepper. Mix with vegetables and bacon. Marinate overnight.

Green Bean and Feta Salad

AN EASY YEAR-ROUND SALAD

Serves 4–6

- 2 pounds fresh green beans
- ½ pound feta cheese, crumbled
- 1 cup chopped walnuts

Vinaigrette:
- 1 tablespoon Dijon mustard
- 4 tablespoons red wine vinegar
- 1 teaspoon sugar
- ½ teaspoon salt
- ½ teaspoon freshly ground pepper
- 2 teaspoons fresh lemon juice
- ¼ cup chopped scallions
- ½ cup olive oil

Cook green beans in boiling salted water for approximately 8 to 10 minutes or until beans are tender but firm. Rinse beans immediately in very cold water.

❧ Blend all vinaigrette ingredients. Toss beans with vinaigrette. Chill marinated beans in refrigerator for at least 8 hours (but not more than 1 day).

❧ Just before serving, add feta cheese and walnuts.

Green Beans and Mushrooms with Walnut Dressing

THE BEST GREEN BEAN SALAD

Serves 6

- 1 pound small green beans
- 1 pound mushrooms
- Juice of 1 lemon
- 2 tablespoons walnuts
- 1 tablespoon Dijon mustard
- 2 tablespoons sherry
- Salt and pepper to taste
- ⅓ cup vegetable oil
- 1 tablespoon tarragon

Cook beans al dente. Refresh in cold water. Slice mushrooms and sprinkle with lemon juice. Purée walnuts, mustard, sherry, vinegar, salt and pepper. Add oil and blend well. Combine green beans with dressing. Sprinkle with tarragon. Chill.

Snow Pea Salad

AN UNUSUAL VEGETABLE MELANGE

Serves 6

½　head cauliflower
7　ounces fresh snow peas, strings removed
1　5-ounce can sliced water chestnuts
2　tablespoons chopped pimento

Dressing:

⅓　cup vegetable oil
2　tablespoons lemon juice
1　tablespoon white vinegar
1　tablespoon sugar
½　garlic clove, crushed
½　teaspoon salt
3　tablespoons toasted sesame seeds

Break cauliflower into small florets. In large bowl, combine snow peas and cauliflower. Set aside.

❧　For dressing, mix together all ingredients. Pour over cauliflower and snow peas. Add water chestnuts and pimento. Toss and refrigerate until serving time.

Wild Rice Salad

A CRUNCHY COMPLEMENT
TO COLD POULTRY

Serves 8

1　cup wild rice
1¼　cups chicken stock
1　clove garlic
3　tablespoons butter
1　bunch scallions, sliced
½　pound mushrooms, sliced
3　strips bacon, cooked crisp and crumbled
½　cup chopped stuffed green olives

Dressing:

⅓　cup olive oil
3　tablespoons tarragon vinegar
½　teaspoon marjoram
　　Salt and pepper to taste

Soak rice in cold water overnight.

❧　Simmer rice and garlic clove in chicken stock until liquid is absorbed, approximately 30 minutes. Discard garlic. Pour rice into large bowl and let cool.

❧　Sauté scallions and mushrooms in butter. Add to rice. Add bacon and olives.

❧　To make dressing, combine all ingredients and blend well. Pour over rice mixture. Chill overnight. Serve cold in tomato shells or on a bed of Boston lettuce leaves.

Orange Cashew Chicken Salad

A DEPARTURE FROM TRADITIONAL
CHICKEN SALAD

Serves 4

- ¼ cup cilantro or parsley
- ¼ cup safflower oil
- ¼ cup orange juice
- 2 teaspoons red wine vinegar
- 1½ teaspoons Dijon mustard
- 1 egg
- 1 tablespoon sugar
- ½ teaspoon salt
  Dash Tabasco
- 4 boned chicken breast halves, poached
- 1 head romaine lettuce, torn
- 3 celery stalks, julienned
- 1 red pepper, julienned
- 3 scallions, sliced
- ½ cup cashews
  Orange slices (optional)

Blend cilantro, oil, orange juice, vinegar, mustard, egg, sugar, salt and Tabasco in a blender or food processor.

❦ Cut chicken into ¼″ slices and toss with dressing. Refrigerate 4 to 6 hours or overnight.

❦ When ready to serve, toss chicken and dressing with vegetables and cashews. Garnish with orange slices, if desired.

Chinese Chicken Salad with Honey Sesame Crisps

A MAIN COURSE SALAD WITH
AN ORIENTAL FLAVOR

Serves 4

- ½ package rice sticks, broken into 3″ pieces
  Oil for frying
- 3 cups cooked and shredded chicken
- ½ cup chopped scallions
- 1 large head iceberg lettuce, chopped
- ½ cup toasted slivered almonds
- 2 tablespoons lightly toasted sesame seeds
- 1 cup julienned snow peas
- ½ cup water chestnuts

Chinese Honey Dressing:

- ½ teaspoon dry mustard
- 2 tablespoons honey
- 2 tablespoons sugar
- 1 tablespoon soy sauce
- 2 tablespoons sesame oil
- ½ cup salad oil
- ¼ cup rice vinegar

Honey Sesame Crisps:

- 4 pita breads
- 2 teaspoons butter
- 2 teaspoons honey
- ½ teaspoon sesame seeds

Deep fry rice sticks in small batches. They will puff in only a few seconds. If rice sticks are not available, use thinly sliced egg roll wrappers that have been fried.

❦ In large salad bowl, combine all ingredients except rice sticks. Pour Chinese Honey Dressing over salad and toss with rice sticks. Serve with Honey Sesame Crisps.

❦ To make dressing, combine ingredients and shake to blend.

❦ For Honey Sesame Crisps, split pita breads. Combine butter and honey and spread on each half of pita. Sprinkle with sesame seeds. Broil for 1 minute until browned.

Chicken and Tortilla Salad

A SOPHISTICATED SALAD WITH
SOUTH-OF-THE-BORDER FLAIR

Serves 2

2   tablespoons toasted sesame seeds

1   tablespoon white wine vinegar

1   tablespoon Dijon mustard

½   cup vegetable oil
    Salt and pepper to taste

2   chicken breasts, skinned, boned, and sliced
    into ½" strips

½   teaspoon Tabasco
    Tortillas, cut into ¼" strips

1   head romaine lettuce, sliced

½   cup sliced green peppers

Combine sesame seeds, vinegar, mustard, ¼ cup oil, salt and pepper in blender. In bowl, toss chicken with Tabasco and let stand for 15 minutes.

❧   In frying pan, heat remaining ¼ cup oil and fry tortilla strips. Remove tortilla strips and sauté chicken in pan. When cooked, transfer chicken to large bowl and toss with all ingredients. Serve salad slightly warm.

Haupt Garden, Smithsonian Institution

Smoked Turkey Salad

WILD RICE AND AVOCADO BLEND
PERFECTLY WITH SMOKED TURKEY

Serves 8–10

1   cup wild rice

3   cups chicken stock

1   pound smoked turkey, diced

2   avocados, peeled and diced

1   tablespoon lemon juice
    10-ounces sundried tomatoes in oil, diced

¾   cup diced onion

¼   cup red wine vinegar

½   cup olive oil
    Salt and pepper to taste

¼   cup chopped parsley

Bring wild rice and chicken stock to a boil. Cover and simmer 45 minutes. Transfer to bowl and cool. Add smoked turkey.

❧   Sprinkle avocados with lemon juice. Add to rice mixture. Combine remaining ingredients and add to rice mixture. Toss gently. Serve at room temperature.

SUNDAY BRUNCH

CHEDDAR PECAN TOASTS
SMOKED SALMON SPREAD
STRAWBERRY SPINACH SALAD
SHRIMP SOUFFLE
POPPY SEED CAKE

Apple-Roquefort Slaw

THE TYPE OF APPLE MAKES THIS EITHER
TART OR SWEET

Serves 8–12

1 cup mayonnaise
¼ cup olive oil
¼ cup white wine vinegar
   Dash Tabasco
½ teaspoon Worcestershire sauce
   Dash garlic salt
1 head cabbage, chopped
4 large unpeeled apples, chopped
4 celery stalks, chopped
4 ounces Roquefort cheese, crumbled

Combine mayonnaise, oil, vinegar,
Tabasco, Worcestershire and garlic
salt. Combine with cabbage, apples and
celery. Add Roquefort cheese and toss.

Strawberry Spinach Salad

CARAMELIZED PECANS ADD CRUNCH

Serves 4–6

10 ounces fresh spinach
1 cup sliced celery, cut on diagonal
1 pint strawberries

Caramelized Pecans:
1 cup sugar
1 cup pecans

Poppy Seed Dressing:
½ cup sugar
2 teaspoons salt
2 teaspoons dry mustard
⅔ cup vinegar
4 scallions, chopped
2 cups salad oil
3 tablespoons poppy seeds

For caramelized pecans, combine sugar
and pecans in heavy frying pan. Slowly
cook until all sugar has melted onto pecans
and they are browned. Immediately place
on waxed paper. Cool. These can be
prepared ahead.

❧ To make dressing, combine sugar, salt,
mustard, vinegar and scallions in blender.
Slowly add oil. Stir in poppy seeds.
Refrigerate.

❧ Combine spinach, celery, halved
strawberries and caramelized pecans. Coat
with poppy seed dressing. Toss gently.

Grapefruit and Avocado Salad with Lemon Honey Dressing

SWEET DRESSING CONTRASTS WITH THE
TANGY SALAD

Serves 6

   Bibb lettuce leaves
3 grapefruit, peeled and sectioned,
   membranes removed
3 ripe avocados, peeled and sliced lengthwise
5 ounces bleu cheese, crumbled

Lemon Honey Dressing:
   Juice of 3 lemons
½ cup light olive oil or safflower oil
¼ cup honey
2 tablespoons white wine vinegar
1 teaspoon salt
1 teaspoon pepper

Blend dressing ingredients well.
Arrange Bibb lettuce leaves on salad
plates with grapefuit and avocados placed
in an alternating pattern. Sprinkle with
bleu cheese. Drizzle dressing on salad
before serving.

Raspberry Pear Salad

A FRESH FRUIT SALAD WITH
A CREAMY VINAIGRETTE

Serves 4

4   fresh pears, peeled and sliced
½   cup fresh red raspberries
½   cup toasted pecans
1   head of Bibb lettuce

Vinaigrette:

½   cup extra light olive oil
¼   cup raspberry vinegar
1   tablespoon crème frâiche
1   teaspoon sugar

P repare vinaigrette and chill for several
hours. When ready to serve, arrange
the pears attractively on the lettuce. Top
with raspberries and pecans. Drizzle
vinaigrette over all.

Avocado Mold with Salsa

GARNISH WITH SHRIMP TO SERVE AS
AN ENTREE

Serves 8–12

2   envelopes plain gelatin
½   cup cold water
1¼   cups hot water
3   tablespoons lemon juice
1½   teaspoons grated onion
1   clove garlic, minced
1   scant teaspoon salt
4–5   dashes Tabasco, or to taste
3   cups mashed avocados
¾   cup mayonnaise

Salsa:

1   cucumber, peeled, seeded and finely diced
1   red bell pepper, cut into ¼″ cubes
1   medium red onion, diced
2   large fresh tomatoes, seeded and diced
3   tablespoons red wine vinegar
1   tablespoon Worcestershire sauce
1   teaspoon Tabasco
1   teaspoon salt
¼   cup olive oil

S often gelatin in cold water and dissolve
in hot water. Blend in lemon juice,
onion, garlic, salt and Tabasco. Cool. Force
avocado through sieve. Blend with mayonnaise and cooled gelatin and pour into
small greased timbales (or ceramic molds).
Chill until firm. Unmold and garnish with
salsa.

❧ To make salsa, combine all vegetables
with vinegar, Worcestershire sauce,
Tabasco, salt and olive oil. Place ⅓ of
mixture in food processor and purée about
1 minute. Stir purée into remaining
vegetable mixture and refrigerate for at
least 1 hour.

Bleu Cheese Dressing

A CLASSIC RECIPE

Yields 2½ cups

1   **cup sour cream**
1   **cup mayonnaise**
½   **teaspoon dry mustard**
½   **teaspoon pepper**
½   **teaspoon salt**
2   **teaspoons Worcestershire sauce**
4   **ounces bleu cheese, crumbled**

Blend first 6 ingredients. Add crumbled bleu cheese. Stir another 1 to 2 minutes.

❧ Refrigerate 24 hours before serving.

Basil Seafood Salad

A SAVORY SEAFOOD MEDLEY

Serves 8

4   **cups water**
1   **cup white wine**
1   **teaspoon salt**
1   **teaspoon white pepper**
1   **pound medium shrimp, peeled and deveined**
1   **pound bay scallops**
3   **squid, cleaned and sliced into rings**
2   **tablespoons lemon juice**
½   **cup olive oil**
1   **bunch scallions, thinly sliced**
⅓   **cup fresh basil, sliced across the grain**
1   **head green leaf lettuce, torn into bite-size pieces**
½   **pound radicchio, julienned**

Place water, wine, ½ teaspoon salt and ½ teaspoon pepper in saucepan. Bring to a boil. Cover, reduce heat and let simmer for 5 minutes.

❧ Poach shrimp in simmered liquid until they just turn pink; remove shrimp and set aside. Poach bay scallops in same liquid for 1 minute; remove and set aside. Poach squid for 1 minute; remove and set aside.

❧ In separate bowl make vinaigrette by whisking olive oil into lemon juice. Add scallions, basil, ½ teaspoon salt and ½ teaspoon pepper. Mix well.

❧ Toss ½ cup of the vinaigrette with the seafood. Marinate for 30 minutes.

❧ Before serving, toss remaining vinaigrette with lettuce. Divide lettuce among 8 plates and top with marinated seafood.

Supreme Salad Dressing

A DEPARTURE FROM THE USUAL
VINAIGRETTE

Yields ½ cup

1   egg
1   tablespoon Parmesan cheese
½   teaspoon salt
    White pepper to taste
2   tablespoons Dijon mustard
3   tablespoons lemon juice
1   teaspoon Worcestershire sauce
1   teaspoon sugar
¼   cup oil

Blend all ingredients except oil. Add oil gradually and beat thoroughly.

Spa Vinaigrette

A LIGHT, FLAVORFUL DRESSING

Yields ½ cup

2   tablespoons safflower oil
2   tablespoons rice wine vinegar
2   tablespoons sparkling mineral water
1½ tablespoons lime juice
1   tablespoon grainy mustard
2   tablespoons minced shallots
1   tablespoon chopped chives
    White pepper to taste

Combine all ingredients in bowl and whisk together.

Creamy Bacon Dressing

PERFECT TOSSED WITH ANY
MIXTURE OF GREENS

Yields ½ cup

3   tablespoons sugar
3   tablespoons cider vinegar
2   teaspoons chopped onion
¼   cup mayonnaise
¼   cup sour cream
5   slices bacon, cooked crisp and crumbled

Combine sugar, vinegar and onion. Stir well to dissolve sugar. Whisk in mayonnaise and sour cream until smooth. Add bacon and stir.

❧ Store covered in refrigerator.

SEAFOOD

Poached Red Snapper
with Leeks

VERMOUTH AND LEEKS IMPART A
CONTINENTAL FLAVOR

Serves 4

½ cup butter

6 shallots, minced

4 red snapper fillets, skin on, about 2 pounds

Salt and pepper to taste

5 leeks, bulbs only, julienned

2 cups dry vermouth

¼ cup chopped parsley

Paprika to taste

Melt 6 tablespoons butter in skillet large enough to hold fillets without overlapping. Add shallots and fillets, skin side down. Season with salt and pepper. Add leeks and vermouth. Bring to a boil, reduce heat, cover and simmer for 7 to 8 minutes.

❧ With slotted spatula, carefully lift fillets to heated serving platter or warm plates and keep warm.

❧ Cook liquid mixture, uncovered, over high heat until sauce is reduced by half. Stir in remaining butter and pour over fillets. Garnish with parsley and sprinkle with paprika.

Saucy Sole

CHEESE TOPPING CREATES A RICH CRUST

Serves 6

2 pounds fillet of sole

2 tablespoons lemon juice

½ cup grated Parmesan cheese

½ cup shredded mozzarella cheese

½ cup butter, softened

3 tablespoons mayonnaise

½ cup chopped scallions

½ cup sliced mushrooms

Dash of Tabasco

Place fillets in a single layer on well-greased broiler pan. Brush fish with lemon juice.

❧ Combine Parmesan, mozzarella, butter, mayonnaise, scallions, mushrooms and Tabasco.

❧ Broil fish 4 to 6 minutes, until it flakes easily with a fork. Remove fish from heat and spread with cheese mixture. Broil an additional 3 to 4 minutes, or until lightly browned.

Roasted Striped Bass

FROM CHEF MARTIN GARBISU,
THE JOCKEY CLUB, RITZ-CARLTON HOTEL

Serves 1

- 4 unpeeled cloves garlic
- 7 ounce fillet of striped bass (with skin)
    Salt and pepper to taste
    Flour
- 2 ounces olive oil
- 3 bunches fresh thyme, chopped

Blanch garlic in boiling water for 15 minutes or until garlic is soft. Season and flour fish on each side. Sauté garlic in olive oil. When oil is hot, place fish in pan, skin side down.

❧ While cooking fish, spoon pan oils over the top. When fish is brown and crispy, turn fish and continue cooking until done.

❧ Remove fish from pan, saving oil and garlic, and place on a warm plate. Add chopped thyme to hot oil and cook until crispy. Pour hot oil, thyme and garlic over fish and serve immediately.

Baked Bluefish Niçoise

A BLEND OF SUMMER FLAVORS

Serves 2

- ¼ cup olive oil
- 2–3 cloves garlic, minced
- 1 whole clove
- ¼ teaspoon thyme
- 1 teaspoon basil
    Salt and pepper to taste
- ½ teaspoon paprika
- 1 cup dry white wine
- 4 medium tomatoes, chopped
- 1 pound bluefish fillets
- 2 tablespoons sliced ripe olives
- 2 tablespoons capers
- 2 tablespoons chopped parsley
    Lemon wedges

Heat oil in saucepan. Add garlic and cook for 1 to 2 minutes. Add clove, thyme, basil, salt, pepper, paprika, white wine and tomatoes. Simmer 5 minutes.

❧ Arrange bluefish fillets in flat baking dish. Pour sauce over fillets. Sprinkle with olives and capers. Cover with foil and bake at 350 degrees for 15 to 20 minutes, or until fish flakes easily with a fork. Remove foil for last 5 minutes of cooking. Garnish with lemon wedges and parsley.

Marinated Mako

PERFECT FOR GRILLING

Serves 2

    Juice of 3 lemons
- ¾ cup olive oil
- 2 teaspoons oregano
    Salt and pepper to taste
- ½ pound Mako shark

Combine lemon juice, olive oil, oregano, salt and pepper. Place Mako in a baking dish and cover with marinade. Refrigerate at least 30 minutes before cooking.

❧ Grill Mako 4 minutes per side, basting with marinade during grilling.

Sesame-Seeded Fillet of Salmon

FROM CHEF JEFF TUNKS,
THE RIVER CLUB

Serves 4

2   ripe papaya
½   cup white port
1   bunch fresh basil
4   cups heavy cream
    Salt to taste
1   2-pound Norwegian salmon fillet, cut into quarters
2   ounces sesame seeds
¼   cup light olive oil

Peel and remove seeds from papayas. Reserve 1 papaya for garnish. Coarsely chop 1 papaya and place in saucepan with white port and ½ bunch of basil. Simmer until port has almost evaporated. Add heavy cream and reduce by one-third. Purée sauce in food processor or blender. Strain and season with salt. Set aside.

❦ Dredge salmon fillets in sesame seeds. Sauté salmon in olive oil until browned on both sides. Transfer to baking dish and cook at 350 degrees for 5 minutes. Do not overcook.

❦ Quarter reserved papaya and slice each quarter into a fan. Divide sauce among dinner plates. Top each with a salmon fillet and garnish with papaya and sprigs of basil.

Salmon Soufflé

AN UNCOMMON PRESENTATION

Serves 3–4

½   cup clam juice
½   cup milk
3   tablespoons butter
2   tablespoons chopped scallions
3   tablespoons flour
½   teaspoon salt
    Dash of pepper
1   tablespoon tomato paste
½   teaspoon oregano or marjoram
4   egg yolks
¼   pound cooked salmon, flaked
½   cup grated Swiss cheese
5   egg whites

Mix clam juice and milk in saucepan and bring to a boil.

❦ In separate saucepan, sauté scallions in butter. Add flour and cook for 2 minutes. Gradually beat in milk mixture, salt, pepper, tomato paste and oregano or marjoram. Bring to a boil and cook for 1 minute, stirring constantly. Remove from heat.

❦ Beat in egg yolks 1 at a time. Mix in salmon and all but 1 tablespoon grated cheese.

❦ Beat egg whites until stiff. Stir ¼ of egg whites into salmon mixture. Fold in remaining egg whites.

❦ Turn mixture into buttered 6-cup soufflé mold and sprinkle with remaining cheese. A collar may be placed around soufflé dish to prevent overflow.

❦ Place soufflé in middle of preheated 400 degree oven. Immediately reduce oven temperature to 375 degrees and bake for 30 minutes.

Lobster Au Gratin

A CREAMY BLEND OF LOBSTER AND
MUSHROOMS

Serves 4

4   tablespoons butter
2   tablespoons flour
½   teaspoon dry mustard
1½ cups light cream
3   tablespoons Parmesan cheese
    Salt to taste
1   egg yolk, slightly beaten
1   pound cooked lobster meat, cut up
½   cup sliced mushrooms
2   tablespoons sherry (optional)

Melt 2 tablespoons butter and gradually stir in flour and mustard. Add cream. Cook over low heat, stirring constantly, until thickened. Blend in 2 tablespoons cheese and salt to taste.

❦ Mix a little sauce into egg yolk, then stir yolk mixture quickly into sauce. Stir in 1 tablespoon butter. Add lobster meat, mushrooms and sherry.

❦ Spoon into casserole and dot with remaining 1 tablespoon butter. Bake at 400 degrees until browned, approximately 15 minutes.

Sliced Salmon Fillets

SERVE WITH OUR ZUCCHINI SAUTE

Serves 4–6

2   pounds salmon fillets
1¼   cups crème fraîche
1   tablespoon grainy French mustard
3   tablespoons olive oil
2½   pounds ripe tomatoes, peeled, seeded
     and finely chopped
1   teaspoon dried thyme
     Salt and pepper to taste
3   tablespoons dry white wine
3   tablespoons white wine vinegar
1½   tablespoons finely chopped shallots or
     scallions
¾   cup unsalted butter

Lay salmon on cutting board, skin side down. Cut into ½″ thick slices at 30 degree angle. Discard skin. Place salmon in well-greased baking dish. Sprinkle lightly with salt. Refrigerate.

❦ Combine 1 cup crème fraîche with mustard. Set aside.

❦ Heat olive oil in skillet. Sauté tomatoes over medium heat, stirring until thick and well reduced, about 6 to 7 minutes. Add thyme, salt and pepper. Set aside.

❦ Combine wine, vinegar and shallots in non-aluminum saucepan. Boil over medium-high heat until most of liquid is evaporated. Whisk in remaining ¼ cup crème fraîche and reduce by half over high heat. Gradually whisk in butter. When sauce is thick and foamy, combine with reserved tomato mixture. Season to taste and keep warm.

❦ Bake salmon at 500 degrees for 4 minutes.

❦ Warm mustard cream in saucepan or microwave.

❦ Before serving, spoon tomato butter sauce onto warm dinner plates. Place 2 slices salmon on top of sauce. Spoon mustard cream sauce over salmon. Serve immediately.

Salmon Baked in Wine and Tarragon

SIMPLE AND DELICATELY SEASONED

Serves 4

4 salmon steaks
2 tablespoons butter
⅛ teaspoon salt
¼ teaspoon white pepper
2 tablespoons lemon juice
¼ cup white wine
½ teaspoon tarragon

Place salmon steaks in greased baking dish. Rub with butter. Mix remaining ingredients and pour over fish. Bake, uncovered, at 450 degrees until done, approximately 10 minutes per inch of thickness.

Grilled Salmon with Gazpacho Salsa

A SPICY SALMON ENTREE

Serves 4

1 cucumber, peeled, seeded and finely chopped
1 red pepper, chopped
1 medium red onion, chopped
2 large tomatoes, skinned, seeded and chopped
3 tablespoons red wine vinegar
1 tablespoon Worcestershire sauce
1 teaspoon Tabasco
1 teaspoon salt
¼ cup plus 2 tablespoons olive oil
4 salmon steaks, 1″ thick

Combine cucumber, red pepper, onion, tomatoes, vinegar, Worcestershire sauce, Tabasco, salt and ¼ cup olive oil. Place ⅓ of mixture in blender or food processor and purée. Stir purée into remaining vegetables and cover. Set aside for 1 hour.

❦ Rub salmon steaks with remaining 2 tablespoons olive oil and grill over hot coals until steaks are crisp, brown and just cooked through, about 4 minutes each side.

❦ Cut each steak in half lengthwise and place on serving dish. Place spoonful of salsa over each steak. Serve remaining salsa separately.

Ginger Tuna

AN EXOTIC GRILLED DISH

Serves 6

¾ cup light soy sauce
1½ cups orange juice
½ tablespoon minced garlic
½ tablespoon minced ginger
¼ cup olive oil
6 tuna steaks, approximately 1″ thick

Combine soy sauce, orange juice, garlic, ginger and oil. Pour over tuna steaks and marinate for 4 to 6 hours. Grill tuna over hot coals until done, approximately 6 to 8 minutes per side.

Flounder with Dill and Mustard Sauce

JULIENNED VEGETABLES MAKE THIS
A ONE-DISH MEAL

Serves 4

2	teaspoons lemon juice
1½	teaspoons olive or vegetable oil
3	teaspoons chopped fresh dill
3	teaspoons Dijon mustard
½	teaspoon salt
½	teaspoon pepper
¼	teaspoon sugar
½	clove garlic, crushed
	Dash of paprika
2	pounds flounder fillets (or any firm white fish)
2	carrots, julienned
1	small zucchini, julienned
¼	cup Parmesan cheese

Combine lemon juice, oil, dill, mustard, salt, pepper, sugar, garlic and paprika. Brush both sides of fillets with mixture and arrange in flat baking dish.

❦ Layer julienned vegetables over fillets and top with remaining sauce. Sprinkle with Parmesan cheese and additional paprika. Cover and bake at 350 degrees for approximately 15 minutes, or until fish flakes.

Turbot à l'Orange

THE FILLETS ARE PRESENTED IN THEIR
PARCHMENT WRAPPINGS

Serves 6

6	turbot fillets, approximately 6 ounces each
	Salt and pepper to taste
	Peel of 1 orange, finely slivered
	Peel of 1 lemon, finely slivered
2–3	tablespoons chopped scallions

Sauce:

⅔	cup fume blanc, or other dry white wine
⅔	cup chicken or fish stock
½	cup heavy cream
	Sprig of thyme
2	tablespoons butter, softened

Cut 6 pieces parchment paper into heart shapes 12″ long and 10″ at widest point. Butter paper.

❦ Place fillet lengthwise on half of heart-shaped paper and season with salt and pepper. Sprinkle orange peel, lemon peel and scallions on fish.

❦ Fold other half of paper over fish, matching edges. Seal paper by folding edges around fish. Twist tip of heart to complete enclosure. Repeat with each fillet.

❦ Bake at 425 degrees on baking sheet for 7 minutes.

❦ To make sauce, heat wine and stock in saucepan and cook until reduced by half. Add cream and thyme. Continue cooking until slightly thickened. Whisk in butter.

❦ To serve fish, cut cases open by slashing a large X on top of each. Fold back paper and serve with sauce.

Scallops Provençale

FLAVORED WITH TOMATO, MUSHROOMS
AND GARLIC

Serves 4–6

3   tablespoons butter

8   medium mushrooms, sliced

1   large tomato, peeled, seeded and chopped

3   shallots, minced

1   tablespoon chopped parsley

2   cloves garlic, minced

½   teaspoon thyme

2   tablespoons dry white wine

     Salt and pepper to taste

4   tablespoons olive oil

1   pound bay scallops or quartered sea scallops

½   cup flour

Sauté mushrooms in butter. Add tomato, shallots, parsley, garlic, thyme and wine. Simmer 5 minutes. Season with salt and pepper.

❦ Heat oil in skillet. Dredge scallops in flour and sauté quickly over high heat until golden on all sides, approximately 5 minutes.

❦ Place scallops in individual ramekins or shells. Spoon sauce over scallops. Garnish with additional parsley.

Capitol Building

FAMILY SUPPER

MARYLAND CRAB CAKES
DILLICIOUS GREEN BEANS
SAUTEED CHERRY TOMATOES
OLD-FASHIONED STRAWBERRY SHORTCAKE

Broiled Scallops

A SIMPLE WAY TO SERVE FRESH SCALLOPS

Serves 4–6

½ **cup butter**
1 **clove garlic, minced**
2 **pounds bay scallops or quartered sea scallops**
¼ **cup flour**
1 **teaspoon paprika**
    White pepper to taste
    Cayenne pepper to taste

M elt butter with garlic. Pour half of melted butter into shallow baking dish large enough to hold scallops in a single layer. Add scallops.

❧ Combine flour, paprika, white pepper and cayenne. Sprinkle over the scallops and pour remaining butter on top. Broil scallops until golden brown, approximately 8 minutes.

Seafood Strudel

A HEARTY SEAFOOD PASTRY

Serves 6–8

3 **tablespoons minced shallots**
¾ **cup unsalted butter**
2 **tablespoons flour**
½ **teaspoon Dijon mustard**
    Pinch of salt
    Pinch of cayenne pepper
¾ **cup milk, at room temperature**
2 **tablespoons heavy cream**
½ **cup plus 2 tablespoons freshly grated Parmesan cheese**
¼ **teaspoon dry mustard**
½ **pound phyllo pastry sheets**
1 **pound crab, shrimp, lobster or halibut (or combination), cleaned, shelled, cooked and cut into bite-size chunks**
½ **cup grated Swiss cheese**
¾ **cup sour cream**
½ **cup chopped parsley**
2 **tablespoons chopped chives**
1 **large garlic clove, minced**

S auté shallots in 2 tablespoons butter over low heat until soft. Stir in flour and cook, stirring constantly, until mixture just begins to bubble.

❧ Remove from heat and add Dijon mustard, salt and cayenne pepper. Slowly stir in milk. Place over medium heat and cook, stirring constantly, until mixture bubbles and thickens. Remove from heat and add cream. Cover and chill until very thick and firm, about 2 hours.

❧ Combine ½ cup Parmesan cheese and dry mustard in small bowl.

❧ Melt remaining 10 tablespoons of butter. Place 3 sheets of phyllo on buttered baking sheet. Brush with melted butter and sprinkle with Parmesan mixture. Repeat process until all phyllo is used. Layer seafood evenly on phyllo and sprinkle with Swiss cheese. Dot with sour cream. Sprinkle with ¼ cup parsley, chives and garlic and dot with chilled sauce.

❧ Roll up phyllo and brush with melted butter. Bake at 375 degrees for 12 minutes. Remove from oven and brush with additional melted butter.

❧ Slice diagonally with serrated knife into 1 ½″ pieces. Push slices together to reshape loaf. Add remaining ¼ cup parsley to remaining butter and brush again.

Snapper Hachinango
à la Veracruzana

SNAPPER WITH A SOUTHWESTERN TASTE

Serves 4

1   pound red snapper fillets
1   lemon, cut in half
2   tablespoons sesame oil
½   cup finely chopped onion
3   cloves garlic, crushed
1   16-ounce can whole tomatoes, drained and coarsely chopped
3   tablespoons chopped parsley
1   tablespoon vinegar
1   tablespoon red wine
1   tablespoon salt
½   teaspoon oregano
¼   teaspoon thyme
1   teaspoon sugar
¼   cup water
10 large green olives, pitted
2   jalapeño peppers, thinly sliced
2   tablespoons olive oil

Rub fish with lemon. Fry in hot sesame oil for 1 minute on each side. Remove to baking dish.

❧ Sauté onion, garlic and tomatoes in oil for 5 minutes. Add parsley, vinegar, wine, salt, oregano, thyme, sugar and water. Cook an additional 5 minutes.

❧ Cover fish with sauce. Top with olives and peppers. Sprinkle with olive oil and bake at 300 degrees until done, approximately 30 minutes.

Scallop and Zucchini
Béarnaise

AN INNOVATIVE COMBINATION

Serves 6

1   medium zucchini, thinly sliced on the diagonal
3   tablespoons butter
1   pound bay scallops or quartered sea scallops
    Salt and pepper to taste
1   tomato, peeled, seeded and chopped
2   teaspoons olive oil

Béarnaise Sauce:
¼   cup white wine vinegar
2   tablespoons finely chopped shallots
1   tablespoon fresh tarragon or 1 teaspoon dried tarragon
    Salt and pepper to taste
2   egg yolks
1   cup butter
2   tablespoons heavy cream

Blanch zucchini in boiling salted water. Drain and rinse in cold water. Melt butter in pan over medium heat. Sauté scallops until they just turn opaque. Season with salt and pepper. Line the bottom and sides of 6 ramekins with the zucchini. Divide scallops evenly among the ramekins.

❧ Sauté tomato lightly in olive oil. Season with salt and pepper. Set aside.

❧ For the Béarnaise sauce, combine vinegar, shallots, tarragon, salt and pepper. Simmer until the liquid has almost evaporated. Cool for 5 minutes. Over very low heat, whisk egg yolks into mixture until it thickens. Whisk in butter 1 tablespoon at a time. Add the cream.

❧ Pour sauce over scallops. Broil until the top just browns. Garnish with tomato.

Crawfish Etouffée

A CAJUN DISH WORTH THE EFFORT

Serves 6–8

1 **cup butter**
¼ **cup flour**
1 **cup chopped scallions**
1 **cup chopped onions**
2 **cloves garlic, minced**
½ **cup chopped green pepper**
½ **cup chopped celery**
1 **bay leaf**
¼ **teaspoon thyme**
1 **teaspoon basil**

1 **8-ounce can tomato sauce**
½ **teaspoon white pepper**
    Salt to taste
1 **tablespoon Worcestershire sauce**
    Tabasco to taste
1 **cup water**
1 **cup clam juice**
2 **pounds crawfish tails (or raw shrimp)**
1 **tablespoon lemon juice**
1 **tablespoon grated lemon rind**
¼ **cup minced parsley**
½ **cup sliced scallion tops, for garnish**

In heavy pan, melt ½ cup butter and gradually stir in flour. Cook mixture over low heat, stirring frequently, until dark brown in color, approximately 45 minutes.

❦ Add scallions, onions, garlic, green pepper, celery, bay leaf, thyme, basil and remaining ½ cup butter. Sauté 30 minutes.

❦ Add tomato sauce, pepper, salt, Worcestershire sauce, Tabasco, water and

clam juice. Bring to a boil. Reduce heat and simmer 1 hour. Remove bay leaf. The étouffée may be frozen at this point.

❦ Add crawfish tails, lemon juice, lemon rind and parsley. Heat through but do not boil or crawfish will become tough.

❦ Refrigerate overnight so flavors can blend. Remove 1 hour before reheating so étouffée warms to room temperature. Heat through without boiling. Serve over white rice and garnish with scallion tops.

Shrimp Creole

ITALIAN SAUSAGE MAKES THIS EXTRA SPICY

Serves 4

4   links hot Italian sausage, cut into bite-size pieces
1   medium red pepper, chopped
1   medium green pepper, chopped
1   medium onion, chopped
3   cloves garlic, minced
1   28-ounce can tomatoes, including juice
1   bay leaf
1   teaspoon dried basil
1   pound shrimp, shelled and deveined
    Salt and pepper to taste

Sauté sausage; add red and green pepper, onion and garlic and cook until tender. Chop tomatoes and add to mixture, along with juice, bay leaf and basil. Cover and simmer 1½ hours, stirring occasionally.

❧ Just before serving, add shrimp and cook until pink, approximately 3 to 5 minutes. Season with salt and pepper. Serve over rice.

Jambalaya

A CAJUN CLASSIC

Serves 6

½   pound Kielbasa
2   tablespoons olive oil
⅓   cup chopped green pepper
2   cloves garlic, minced
½   cup chopped onion
½   cup chopped parsley
½   cup chopped celery
1   16-ounce can tomatoes
1   cup chicken stock
½   cup chopped scallion
½   teaspoon thyme
1   bay leaf
1   teaspoon oregano
½   teaspoon chili powder
⅛   teaspoon ground cloves
¼   teaspoon cayenne pepper
¼   teaspoon black pepper
1   cup uncooked rice
1½ pounds shrimp, peeled and deveined

Cut sausage into ¼″ slices and sauté in bottom of Dutch oven. Remove from pan and reserve. Add olive oil to sausage drippings and sauté green pepper, garlic, onion, parsley and celery for 5 minutes. Add tomatoes, chicken stock, scallions, seasonings, rice and sausage. Cover and cook over low heat for 30 minutes. Add shrimp and stir until it turns pink. Transfer to oven and bake at 350 degrees for 25 minutes.

Stuffed Shrimp

SHRIMP WITH A ZESTY ITALIAN FLAVOR

Serves 2–4

2   cloves garlic
½   cup vermouth or white wine
1   cup butter
1   cup Italian bread crumbs
1   teaspoon basil
½   teaspoon oregano
½   cup Parmesan cheese
1   pound large raw shrimp, peeled and deveined

Crush garlic cloves and soak in vermouth or wine for 30 minutes. Remove garlic.

❧ Combine ½ cup butter, bread crumbs, basil, oregano and cheese. Add wine gradually until mixture becomes a paste.

❧ Make a deep slit down the back of each shrimp. Fill with paste and place in baking dish.

❧ Bake at 350 degrees for 20 to 25 minutes. Serve drizzled with remaining ½ cup melted butter.

Shrimp en Brochette

SERVE WITH A RICE PILAF

Serves 4–6

⅓ cup fresh lemon juice

2 cloves garlic, minced

1 tablespoon olive oil

2 teaspoons grated ginger

2 dashes Tabasco

1 pound medium shrimp, shelled and deveined

24 small mushrooms

1 small onion, quartered and separated

24 cherry tomatoes

Combine lemon juice, garlic, oil, ginger and Tabasco. Pour over shrimp, mushrooms, onions and tomatoes and marinate in refrigerator overnight.

❧ Heat broiler or grill. Thread shrimp, mushrooms, onions and tomatoes alternately on metal skewers. Reserve marinade.

❧ Broil or grill 3 minutes, turn, and baste with marinade. Continue broiling or grilling 2 to 3 minutes longer until shrimp are pink and opaque. Do not overcook or shrimp will become tough.

Shrimp Soufflé

A DELICATELY FLAVORED ENTREE

Serves 4–6

Butter

Grated Parmesan cheese

⅓ cup butter

⅓ cup flour

1¼ cups milk

¼ cup dry white wine

½ cup shredded Gruyere or Swiss cheese

2 tablespoons chopped parsley

2 cloves garlic, crushed

½ teaspoon paprika

6 eggs, separated

6 ounces small shrimp, cooked, peeled and deveined

½ teaspoon cream of tartar

Butter bottom and sides of 2- to 2½-quart soufflé dish or straight-sided casserole. Dust with Parmesan cheese. Prepare collar by making a 4″ wide band of triple-thickness aluminum foil long enough to go around dish. Butter 1 side of band and dust with Parmesan cheese. Wrap band around dish. Collar should stand at least 2″ above rim of dish. Set aside.

❧ Over medium-high heat, melt ⅓ cup butter and blend in flour. Stir in milk all at once. Cook and stir until mixture boils and is smooth and thickened. Stir in wine. Remove from heat. Stir in Gruyere cheese and seasonings until cheese is melted. Allow to cool slightly. Thoroughly blend egg yolks and shrimp into sauce.

❧ In large mixing bowl, beat egg whites with cream of tartar at high speed just until whites no longer slip when bowl is tilted. Gently but thoroughly fold egg whites into shrimp mixture. Carefully pour into prepared dish.

❧ Bake at 350 degrees until puffy, delicately browned and soufflé shakes slightly when oven rack is moved gently back and forth, about 45 minutes. Quickly but carefully remove collar. Serve immediately.

Shrimp in the Shell

A CASUAL SUPPER DISH

Serves 2–4

½   **cup butter**

1   **tablespoon sesame or vegetable oil**

1   **pound shrimp, unshelled**

⅓   **cup soy sauce**

3   **tablespoons sherry**

1   **clove garlic, crushed**

Melt butter and oil in large skillet and add shrimp. Mix remaining ingredients and add to skillet. Cook over medium heat 3 to 5 minutes or until shrimp turn pink.

Creamy Shrimp Creole

A BLEND OF TWO SAUCES SETS THIS APART

Serves 4

1   **pound shrimp, cooked, peeled and deveined**

1½   **cups cooked rice**

Tomato Sauce:

1   **tablespoon olive oil**

1–2   **cloves garlic**

1   **large onion, chopped**

1   **cup diced celery**

1   **large green pepper, chopped**

1   **28-ounce can tomatoes**

1   **bay leaf**

    Rosemary to taste

    Salt and pepper to taste

White Sauce:

2   **tablespoons butter**

1   **tablespoon flour**

½   **cup milk**

For tomato sauce, sauté garlic in olive oil. Add onions, celery and green pepper and cook until browned. Mash tomatoes and add to mixture. Add bay leaf and rosemary. Simmer 30 to 40 minutes, or until most of liquid is evaporated. Season with salt and pepper.

❧ For white sauce, melt butter in saucepan; whisk in flour. Blend in milk and cook until thick, stirring constantly.

❧ Combine tomato and white sauces and blend well. Add shrimp and heat through. Serve over cooked rice.

Maryland Crab Cakes

THE ULTIMATE SUMMER DISH

Serves 4

1½ tablespoons chopped parsley
     Minced garlic to taste
2   teaspoons Dijon mustard
½   tablespoon sugar
⅓   cup mayonnaise
1   egg
1   pound backfin crabmeat
¼   cup unseasoned breadcrumbs
2   tablespoons butter

Mix together parsley, garlic, mustard, sugar, mayonnaise and egg. Fold in crab and breadcrumbs.

❦ Shape into ¾″ thick, 3″ round cakes.

❦ Sauté in butter until bronwed, then bake at 450 degrees for 10 minutes.

Crab Cakes with Tomato Coulis

FROM CHEF JEFFREY A. BUBEN
OCCIDENTAL RESTAURANT

Serves 3–4

1   pound jumbo lump crabmeat
1   tablespoon Dijon mustard
1   tablespoon Fish Velouté
1   egg
1   tablespoon chopped coriander
1   tablespoon chopped parsley
     Salt and pepper to taste
     Bread crumbs
8   tablespoons sifted flour
     Clarified butter

Remove shells from crabmeat, being careful not to break up lumps. Mix first seven ingredients together, adding just enough crumbs to bind mixture. (Bread crumbs are made from dried french bread, crust removed, and grated on fine grater, then passed through fine sieve. They should be white and textured like fine sand.) Shape into round patties, approximately 2 ounces each.

❦ Dredge in sifted flour and take off excess flour by patting between hands. Sear in very hot pan on both sides in clarified butter until golden brown. Serve topped with Tomato Coulis.

Fish Velouté:

½   cup white wine
½   cup fish stock
2   shallots, minced
16   ounces heavy cream
     Salt and pepper to taste

Reduce wine, shallots and stock until almost dry. Add cream and reduce by one-third. Season to taste and pass through fine strainer. Store in refrigerator until ready to use.

Tomato Coulis:

2   slices bacon
3   shallots
3   cloves garlic
1½   cups tomato purée
2   tablespoons tomato paste
2   cups chicken stock
1   bay leaf
4   sprigs of thyme
     Salt and pepper to taste

In large saucepan, cook bacon until crisp. Add shallots and garlic; sauté briefly. Add tomato purée, paste and chicken stock. Add herbs, salt and pepper. Cook slowly until reduced by one-third. Pass through fine strainer and correct seasoning to taste.

Crab Cakes

FROM CHEF MARTIN GARBISU,
THE JOCKEY CLUB, RITZ-CARLTON HOTEL

Serves 2

1 **pound jumbo lump crabmeat**
1 **egg**
2 **teaspoons mustard**
1 **teaspoon Worcestershire sauce**
  Salt and pepper
  Fresh bread crumbs
  Flour
  Clarified butter
2 **tablespoons unsalted butter**
2 **teaspoons chopped parsley**
1 **teaspoon lemon juice**

Remove shells from crabmeat. Mix together egg, mustard and Worcestershire sauce. Salt and pepper to taste. Add egg mixture to crab. Add enough bread crumbs to mixture to bind so you can make cakes with your hands.

❧ Flour the cakes on both sides and sauté in clarified butter. Brown 1 side, turn and immediately place in a 350 degree oven. Bake for 4 minutes or until center is just warm.

❧ Melt unsalted butter and heat until butter foams. Add parsley and lemon juice and stir briefly. Pour over crabcakes.

Crab Cakes with Basil Tartar Sauce

THE SAUCE IS A REFRESHING CONTRAST
TO THE CRAB

Serves 4

1 **egg plus 1 egg yolk**
3 **tablespoons heavy cream**
1 **teaspoon lemon juice**
½ **teaspoon pepper**
½ **teaspoon dry mustard**
½ **teaspoon salt**
½ **teaspoon Worcestershire sauce**
1 **tablespoon chopped shallots**
2 **tablespoons chopped scallions**
2 **tablespoons chopped fresh parsley**
2 **tablespoons cracker crumbs**
1 **pound lump crabmeat**
¼ **cup dry bread crumbs**
2 **tablespoons clarified butter**

Combine eggs, cream, lemon juice, pepper, mustard, salt, Worcestershire sauce, shallots, scallions, parsley, cracker crumbs and crabmeat.

❧ Divide mixture into 8 equal portions and shape into patties. Sprinkle bread crumbs on both sides. Place on greased cookie sheet and drizzle with clarified butter. Refrigerate at least 1 hour.

❧ Bake at 475 degrees until lightly browned, approximately 10 minutes.

Basil Tartar Sauce:
½ **cup fresh basil**
½ **cup mayonnaise**
1 **tablespoon sour cream**
1 **teaspoon lemon juice**
1 **teaspoon minced garlic**
  Salt, pepper and Tabasco to taste

Combine all ingredients. Mix well. Serve with crab cakes.

MEATS & POULTRY

Steak à la Moutarde

COGNAC AND MUSTARD COMBINE
FOR A WONDERFUL SAUCE

Serves 4

4 beef tenderloins, approximately 8 ounces
each

Salt and pepper to taste

2 tablespoons butter

2 tablespoons finely chopped shallots

2 tablespoons cognac or brandy

¼ cup chicken stock

3 tablespoons Dijon or coarse mustard

2 tablespoons chopped fresh parsley

Season beef with salt and pepper. Heat large skillet until very hot. Sear tenderloins for 4 minutes, then turn and cook an additional 4 to 6 minutes or until they reach desired doneness. Remove beef from pan and keep warm. Melt butter in pan and sauté shallots 2 to 3 minutes. Add cognac and stock. Bring to a boil and stir in mustard. Pour sauce over beef and garnish with parsley.

Flank Steak Fajitas

A SUMMER MEAL FOR THE FAMILY

Serves 6

¼ cup olive oil

¼ cup white wine vinegar

3 cloves garlic, minced

½ teaspoon salt

½ teaspoon oregano

⅛ teaspoon pepper

4 scallions, chopped

1 flank steak, approximately 1½ pounds

12 flour tortillas

Salsa, guacamole and sour cream for
topping

Combine oil, vinegar, garlic, salt, oregano, pepper and scallions. Score meat and marinate, covered, at least 6 hours or overnight.

❧ Grill steak to desired doneness. Heat tortillas in iron skillet until light brown. To keep warm, wrap in damp cloth and place in 275-degree oven.

❧ Slice meat across grain and place on tortillas. Top with salsa, guacamole and sour cream.

Grilled Beef Tenderloin

SESAME SEEDS ADD
NUTTY FLAVOR

Serves 8–10

- ¾ cup soy sauce
- ¼ cup vegetable oil
- ¼ cup flour
- ½ cup sugar
- ½ cup toasted sesame seeds
- 2 scallions, sliced
- 2 cloves garlic, crushed
- ¼ teaspoon pepper
- 4 pounds beef tenderloin, sliced into fillets

Combine all ingredients except meat and blend well. Pour over fillets and marinate at least 1 hour. Grill fillets, to desired doneness, basting with marinade.

Oriental Flank Steak

THE MARINADE CAN BE USED
WITH OTHER MEATS

Serves 6–8

- ¾ cup vegetable oil
- ¼ cup soy sauce
- 3 tablespoons honey
- 2 tablespoons wine vinegar
- 1 tablespoon grated fresh ginger
- 1 teaspoon pepper
- 2 cloves garlic, crushed
- 4 scallions, finely chopped
- 1 flank steak, approximately 2 pounds

Combine oil, soy sauce, honey, vinegar, ginger, pepper, garlic and scallions. Score meat and marinate, covered, in refrigerator at least 4 hours or overnight.

❧ Grill or broil steak to desired doneness.

Roast on the Rocks

ROCK SALT MAKES A SAVORY CRUST

Serves 6–8

- 1 3-pound eye of round roast
- 2–3 cloves garlic, slivered
  Vegetable oil
  Rock salt

Make slits in meat and insert garlic slivers. Rub meat with oil and roll to coat in rock salt. Place meat directly on hot coals. Grill 15 minutes, then turn a third of the way over and grill 13 minutes. Turn to cook final side for 11 minutes. Remove from grill, scrape off loose salt, slice and serve.

Teriyaki Steak Kebabs

- ³/₁ **cup pineapple juice**
- 2 **tablespoons soy sauce**
- 2 **tablespoons lemon juice**
- 2 **cloves garlic, crushed**
- 1 **bay leaf**
- 2 **tablespoons grated ginger**
- 1 **flank steak**

Combine all ingredients except meat. Cut steak into diagonal strips. Marinate at least 4 hours. Thread steak strips onto skewers and grill, basting occasionally with marinade.

❦ For extra color and flavor, alternate red pepper strips, small white onions and mushroom caps with steak on skewers.

Hunan Beef

- 1 **3–4 pound beef roast**
- 3 **tablespoons soy sauce**
- 4 **teaspoons cornstarch**
- 1 **teaspoon sugar**
- 5 **tablespoons vegetable oil**
- 1 **red pepper, sliced in thin strips**
- 1 **green pepper, sliced in thin strips**
- 1 **head broccoli, cut in bite-size pieces**
- 4 **cloves garlic**
- 3 **teaspoons grated fresh ginger**
- 1 **teaspoon red pepper flakes (or to taste)**
- 1 **tomato, peeled, seeded and chopped**

Sauce:

- 3 **tablespoons red wine**
- 2 **tablespoons soy sauce**
- 2 **tablespoons sugar**
- 1½ **tablespoons hoisin sauce**
- 1 **tablespoon cornstarch**
- ³/₄ **teaspoon vegetable oil**

Trim roast of all fat. Freeze. Allow to thaw 1 hour. Slice beef into paper-thin slices. Combine soy sauce, cornstarch, sugar and 1 tablespoon oil. Marinate beef in mixture for at least 4 hours.

❦ Stir together all sauce ingredients.

❦ Heat wok on medium-high setting. Coat bottom with 1 tablespoon oil. Cook peppers and broccoli about 3 minutes. Set vegetables aside. Heat remaining 3 tablespoons oil. Add garlic, ginger, red pepper flakes and beef. Cook until beef loses its pink color. Add cooked vegetables, tomato and sauce. Simmer until sauce thickens. Serve immediately over rice.

Beef Tenderloin du Chef

RICH MUSHROOM SAUCE
TOPS THIS BEEF

Serves 6–8

1   larded beef tenderloin, about 3 pounds
3   slices bacon, diced
¼   cup butter
2   cups diced mushrooms
½   cup minced parsley
¼   cup minced scallions
2   tablespoons brandy

Roast tenderloin at 450 degrees for 30 to 40 minutes or until desired doneness. Cook bacon until crisp and reserve.

❦ Sauté mushrooms, parsley and scallions in butter until lightly browned. Add brandy and heat through. Stir in bacon.

❦ Cut tenderloin on an angle into 1″ thick slices. Spoon warm mushroom sauce over each slice.

Ragout of Beef with Walnuts

A REFRESHINGLY
SEASONED STEW

Serves 4

1½ pounds stew meat or sirloin tips
2   tablespoons bacon drippings
12 pearl onions, peeled
2   rounded tablespoons flour
⅔   cup red wine
1   tablespoon bouquet garni
2   cloves garlic, crushed
2–3 cups beef stock
    Salt and pepper to taste
1   tablespoon butter
4   stalks celery, sliced
2   ounces halved walnuts
1   tablespoon julienned orange rind, white removed

Cut beef into 2″ cubes. Heat ovenproof casserole and add bacon drippings. When pan starts to smoke, add meat and stir until golden. Remove meat, add onions to pan and sauté slowly until browned. Drain all but 1 tablespoon liquid. Sprinkle flour over onions and stir until lightly browned.

❦ Return meat to casserole. Add wine, bouquet garni and garlic. Add enough stock to cover meat. Season with salt and pepper. Bring to a boil. Cover and bake at 325 degrees for 1½ to 2 hours. Casserole can be prepared in advance up to this point.

❦ Just before serving, heat butter in pan. Stir in celery slices and walnuts and cook for 5 minutes. Spoon celery mixture over casserole and sprinkle with orange rind.

Veal Chops with Herb Mustard Butter

VARY THE HERBS FOR
DIFFERENT FLAVORS

Serves 4–6

6 veal chops, approximately 2″ thick
8 ounces whipped unsalted butter
3 teaspoons chopped fresh sage or other fresh herbs
2 teaspoons honey mustard

Broil veal chops, approximately 9 minutes per side. Blend together butter, sage and mustard. Just before serving, top each chop with a dollop of butter mixture.

Summery Veal Cutlets

ACCOMPANY WITH OUR
ROASTED GARLIC POTATOES

Serves 6

1 small head radicchio
1 bunch watercress
⅓ cup oil and vinegar dressing
1 bunch basil
1 egg
6 veal cutlets
2 plum tomatoes, thinly sliced
   Salt to taste
⅔ cup bread crumbs
½ cup grated Romano or Parmesan cheese
3 tablespoons olive oil

Tear radicchio and watercress into bite-size pieces and toss with dressing. Arrange on serving platter and refrigerate.

❧ Remove basil leaves from sprigs. In pie plate, beat egg with 1 tablespoon water. Pound veal cutlets to ⅛″ thickness. Cut each cutlet in half. Arrange basil leaves and tomatoes in center of half of veal. Sprinkle with salt. Place other half of veal on top to form packets. Pound edges to seal.

❧ Combine breadcrumbs and cheese. Dip veal into beaten egg and roll in bread crumb mixture.

❧ Heat 3 tablespoons of oil in skillet over medium-high heat. Cook veal packets until browned, about 2 to 4 minutes per side, adding more oil if necessary. Arrange veal on radicchio and watercress.

Veal Marengo

A SUBTLE STEW

Serves 4

2   pounds veal roast, cut into 1½″ cubes
½   teaspoon pepper
4   tablespoons butter
1   onion, chopped
1   clove garlic, minced
¼   cup flour
1½   cups chicken stock
½   cup dry white wine
1   cup coarsely chopped tomatoes
2–3 sprigs fresh parsley or dill
1   bay leaf
10–12 pearl onions, peeled
1   cup pitted ripe olives (optional)
     Chopped parsley or dill for garnish

Pepper meat. Brown veal cubes, a few at a time, in melted butter. Add chopped onion and garlic to meat and cook over medium heat until onions are translucent. Sprinkle flour over mixture and cook until lightly browned. Gradually stir in stock and wine. Bring mixture to a boil.

❧ Add tomatoes, parsley and bay leaf. Cover and simmer over low heat for 1 hour. Add pearl onions and olives and cook 45 minutes.

❧ Garnish with parsley or dill.

Veal Marsala

ACCOMPANY WITH ONE OF
OUR PASTA DISHES

Serves 4

4 veal scallops, approximately 6 ounces each
2 tablespoons butter
2 tablespoons Marsala wine
4 tablespoons cream
  Salt to taste
  White pepper to taste
  Lemon juice to taste

Place veal scallops between 2 sheets of wet waxed paper and pound with mallet or rolling pin.

❦ Melt butter in frying pan and brown scallops lightly, approximately 2 to 3 minutes per side. Transfer to warm plate.

❦ Add Marsala to pan, stir and bring to a boil. Reduce heat and add cream. Season sauce well with salt, pepper and a few drops of lemon juice. Return veal to pan and heat through.

Vitello Tonnato

RICH AND UNUSUAL

Serves 8

1 5-pound boned breast of veal or veal roast
2 7-ounce cans tuna packed in oil
3 tablespoons vegetable oil
2 cloves garlic, crushed
2 onions, coarsely chopped
2 carrots, coarsely chopped
2 celery stalks, chopped
¼ cup chopped parsley
2 bay leaves
½ teaspoon thyme
2 tablespoons salt
  Pepper to taste
2 cups chicken stock
1 2-ounce can flat anchovy fillets, drained
6 tablespoons lemon juice
4 tablespoons capers
1 lemon, thinly sliced

Blender Mayonnaise:

2 eggs
2 tablespoons lemon juice
1 tablespoon vinegar
½ teaspoon dry mustard
1 teaspoon salt
1½ cups vegetable oil

Drain oil from tuna into Dutch oven. Add vegetable oil and garlic and lightly brown veal. Remove meat and set aside.

❦ Place onions, carrots and celery in pot and cook, stirring frequently, for 5 minutes or until onion is translucent. Add parsley, bay leaves, thyme, salt, pepper, chicken stock, tuna, anchovies and 2 tablespoons lemon juice. Stir well to dissolve any particles that stick to bottom of pan. Bring mixture to a boil. Add veal, reduce heat and cover. Simmer 3 hours, stirring occasionally. Remove veal from pot and allow to cool to room temperature. Chill in refrigerator.

❦ For mayonnaise, combine eggs, lemon juice, vinegar, mustard and salt in blender and blend at high speed for 30 seconds. With blender running at medium speed, slowly add oil in a thin, steady stream. Blend until thick and smooth.

❦ Cook tuna mixture, stirring frequently, until reduced to about 4 cups. Transfer mixture to blender or processor and purée. Combine 2 cups puréed mixture with 2 cups mayonnaise, 4 tablespoons lemon juice and 2 tablespoons capers. Refrigerate.

❦ To serve, slice veal thinly and arrange on large platter. Spoon half of tuna-mayonnaise sauce over veal and garnish with lemon slices and remaining capers. Serve with remaining sauce.

Veal Gerald

MEDITERRANEAN-STYLE VEAL

Serves 4

4   veal cutlets, approximately ¼″ thick
1   cup flour
1   teaspoon salt
½   teaspoon pepper
2   tablespoons butter
¼   cup olive oil
1½ cups Marsala wine
1½ cups sliced mushrooms
4   large slices tomato
4   slices mozzarella cheese

Pound veal until ⅛″ thick. Combine flour with salt and pepper. Dredge veal in flour, shaking off any excess. Melt butter with oil in large skillet. Sauté veal quickly on high heat until browned, about 2 to 3 minutes on each side. Place in warm oven.

❦ Add wine and mushrooms to pan and bring to a boil. Scrape the bottom of pan to loosen any browned bits. Reduce the mixture by half, cooking about 6 to 8 minutes.

❦ Reduce heat and add veal. Place 1 slice tomato, then 1 slice cheese, on each veal scallop. Simmer gently until cheese just begins to melt. Serve at once with sauce spooned over veal.

Broiled Veal Chops in Mustard Caper Sauce

THE SAUCE PROVIDES A PEPPERY ACCENT

Serves 4

4   veal chops, approximately 1″ thick
    Salt and pepper to taste
4   tablespoons lemon juice
1   tablespoon olive oil
2   tablespoons Dijon mustard
6   cloves garlic, minced
¼   cup vermouth
¼   cup chicken stock
1   tablespoon grated lemon peel
2   tablespoons light soy sauce
1   tablespoon sugar
¼   teaspoon Szechuan pepper
3   tablespoons butter
1   tablespoon minced fresh ginger
1   tablespoon cornstarch mixed with cold water
2   tablespoons capers

Lightly salt and pepper veal chops. Combine 2 tablespoons lemon juice, olive oil, 1 tablespoon mustard and 3 cloves garlic. Rub mixture onto chops and set aside.

❦ Combine vermouth, stock, lemon peel, soy sauce, sugar, Szechuan pepper, remaining 2 tablespoons lemon juice and 1 tablespoon mustard. Set aside.

❦ Broil veal chops approximately 5 minutes on each side, allowing centers to remain lightly pink.

❦ While veal is cooking, melt 2 tablespoons butter and sauté ginger and remaining 3 cloves minced garlic. Add vermouth mixture and bring to a boil. Reduce heat and gradually stir in cornstarch mixture until sauce thickens. Remove from heat and stir in remaining 1 tablespoon butter and capers.

❦ Place veal on heated plates and top with sauce.

Grilled Lamb Kebabs

GREAT FOR SUMMER ENTERTAINING

Serves 4–6

2 tablespoons rosemary
4 large cloves garlic, crushed
2 small shallots, minced
1 tablespoon Dijon mustard
2 teaspoons salt
1 teaspoon pepper
1 tablespoon Worcestershire sauce
½ cup red wine vinegar
1 cup olive oil
2 pounds boned leg of lamb

Combine all ingredients except meat.

❧ Cut lamb into 2″ cubes and coat in marinade. Cover and refrigerate at least 8 hours or overnight.

❧ Prepare grill or preheat broiler. Drain and reserve marinade. Skewer meat, leaving small space between cubes to ensure even cooking.

❧ Grill or broil 10 to 15 minutes, turning and basting frequently with reserved marinade.

Lamb with Herbed Sour Cream

SOUR CREAM CREATES A DELICIOUS, CRUSTY COATING

Serves 6–8

1 cup sour cream
3 cloves garlic, minced
2 tablespoons chopped fresh parsley
1 teaspoon crumbled rosemary
1 teaspoon oregano
   Salt and pepper to taste
1 6-pound leg of lamb, boned and butterflied

Combine all ingredients except leg of lamb. Coat lamb with mixture, cover loosely with waxed paper and refrigerate at least 6 hours.

❧ Grill or broil to desired doneness.

Glazed Leg of Lamb

A DELIGHTFULLY SIMPLE WAY TO SERVE LAMB

Serves 8–10

1 8-pound leg of lamb
3 cloves garlic, slivered
1 tablespoon rosemary, crushed
1 tablespoon sage leaves, crushed
1 teaspoon salt
1 teaspoon pepper
¾ cup dry sherry
½ cup currant jelly
½ cup catsup
1 teaspoon crushed marjoram

Make several slits in leg of lamb and insert garlic slivers.

❧ Combine rosemary, sage, salt and pepper. Rub generously into meat.

❧ Combine sherry, jelly, catsup and marjoram. Stir over low heat until heated through. Set aside.

❧ Place lamb on rack in roasting pan. Bake at 325 degrees for 20 to 25 minutes per pound. During last 1½ hours of cooking, baste lamb frequently with sherry mixture. Reheat any remaining sauce and serve with lamb.

Pork Tenderloin with Stilton and Port

THIS DRAMATIC SAUCE MAY ALSO
ACCOMPANY A BEEF TENDERLOIN

Serves 6–8

2   **pork tenderloins, approximately 1 pound each**

2   **tablespoons vegetable oil**

2   **cups port wine**

1   **cup chicken stock**

1   **cup heavy cream**

6–8   **ounces Stilton cheese**

Heat oil in large skillet. Add pork and brown on all sides. Transfer pork to covered roasting pan. Deglaze skillet with port and reduce by half. Add chicken stock and bring to a boil. Pour over pork and bake at 450 degrees until done, approximately 15 minutes. Remove pork and keep warm. Reduce liquid by half and slowly stir in cream. Cook over medium heat until sauce thickens. Add Stilton and stir to blend. Spoon sauce over sliced tenderloin.

Chinese Pork and Walnuts

AUTHENTIC AND FLAVORFUL

Serves 4

1   **teaspoon cornstarch**

1   **tablespoon water**

1   **egg white**

1   **pound boneless pork, cut into 1″ cubes**

3   **tablespoons soy sauce**

1   **tablespoon bourbon**

½   **teaspoon sugar**

4   **tablespoons vegetable oil**

5   **scallions, cut into 2″ slices**

1   **can sliced water chestnuts**

1   **teaspoon minced fresh ginger**

1   **clove garlic, minced**

¾   **cup chopped walnuts**

Mix cornstarch, water and egg white. Add pork and toss until thoroughly coated. Combine soy sauce, bourbon and sugar and set aside.

❧ Heat skillet or wok and add 2 tablespoons oil. Stir-fry pork for 5 minutes or until completely cooked. Remove from pan.

❧ Add remaining 2 tablespoons oil to pan. Stir-fry scallions, water chestnuts, ginger and garlic for 1 minute.

❧ Return pork to pan. Add soy-bourbon mixture and cook quickly until sauce thickens. Stir in walnuts and serve over rice.

Pork Tenderloin with Bourbon Marinade

A BUFFET OR PICNIC ROAST

Serves 6–8

⅓   **cup Worcestershire sauce**

⅓   **cup bourbon**

⅓   **cup soy sauce**

2   **pork tenderloins, approximately 1 pound each**

Combine Worcestershire sauce, bourbon and soy sauce. Marinate, covered in refrigerator, for at least 6 hours or overnight, turning meat several times.

❧ Place meat and marinade in a roasting pan. Roast at 350 degrees until temperature of meat reaches 150 degrees on meat thermometer, approximately 30 to 40 minutes. Baste occasionally.

❧ Slice tenderloin and serve hot with marinade drizzled over top, or cool to room temperature and serve with a honey mustard or flavored mayonnaise.

Herbed Pork Roast

A SUCCULENT, HERB-CRUSTED
ROAST

Serves 6

2 tablespoons sugar
1 tablespoon sage leaves
1½ tablespoons marjoram
1 teaspoon salt
½ teaspoon celery seed
½ teaspoon dry mustard
¼ teaspoon pepper
1 2-pound boneless pork roast

Combine seasonings in small bowl, halving the amounts if dried herbs are used. Rub pork roast thoroughly with mixture. Cover roast with plastic wrap and let stand in refrigerator at least 4 hours or overnight.

❧ Unwrap meat and place on rack in shallow pan. Roast at 325 degrees, allowing about 40 minutes per pound.

Spicy Pork with Egg Noodles

ADD STIR-FRIED BROCCOLI
AS A SIDE DISH

Serves 4–6

¼ cup chicken stock
3 teaspoons sesame oil
2 teaspoons chili paste with garlic
1 tablespoon soy sauce
2 tablespoons rice wine
2 teaspoons hoisin sauce
3 tablespoons peanut oil
1 clove garlic, minced
1 pound ground pork
4 scallions, chopped
1 pound Chinese egg noodles
1 cucumber, peeled, seeded and cut into strips
½ cup bean sprouts

Combine chicken stock, 2 teaspoons sesame oil, chili paste, soy sauce, rice wine and hoisin sauce. Set aside.

❧ Brown garlic and pork in peanut oil over medium heat. Stir in scallions and chicken stock mixture. Simmer over low heat for 3 to 4 minutes, or until thick.

❧ Cook noodles according to package directions, then drain. Toss with remaining teaspoon sesame oil. Pour pork mixture on top of noodles and garnish with cucumbers and bean sprouts.

Chicken Kiev

THE PERFECT DISH FOR A
SIT-DOWN DINNER

Serves 4

½ cup plus 3 tablespoons butter
Juice and grated peel of 1 lemon
2 tablespoons minced parsley
1 teaspoon crushed thyme
2 whole chicken breasts, halved, skinned and boned
Salt and pepper to taste
1 cup flour
1 egg, beaten
1 cup cracker meal

Melt ½ cup butter with lemon juice, grated lemon peel, parsley and thyme. Chill in small bowl until firm.

❧ Pound chicken breasts between waxed paper. Season with salt and pepper.

❧ Place tablespoon of chilled butter mixture in center of each breast and roll breast around butter mixture. (Secure with toothpick if necessary.) Coat with flour, dip into beaten egg and roll in cracker meal. Place chicken in shallow casserole and refrigerate 2 to 3 hours.

❧ Melt 3 tablespoons butter and drizzle over chicken breasts. Bake at 400 degrees for 35 to 40 minutes.

Chicken Dijonnaise

SERVE WITH OUR PECAN PILAF

Serves 4

1 **cup clarified butter**
2 **whole chicken breasts, halved, skinned and boned**
½ **cup flour**
½ **cup thinly sliced onion**
½ **cup sliced mushrooms**
2 **cloves garlic, minced**
4 **artichoke hearts, quartered**
½ **cup heavy cream**
4 **teaspoons Dijon mustard**
⅔ **cup dry vermouth**
   Chopped parsley for garnish

Heat butter in skillet. Lightly dredge chicken breasts in flour. Sauté chicken in butter until lightly browned. Add onions, mushrooms, garlic and artichoke hearts while browning the second side.

❧ Stir over medium heat until reduced by half. Reduce heat and add cream. Stir in mustard and vermouth. Cook until sauce thickens slightly, approximately 3 to 4 minutes.

❧ Remove chicken breasts to serving dish. Pour sauce over chicken and garnish with parsley.

Residence of the Belgian Ambassador

INTERNATIONAL DINNER

SCALLOPS WITH PERNOD AND LEEKS
NORWEGIAN STUFFED CHICKEN
GARLIC ROASTED POTATOES
MIXED GREENS WITH SPA VINAIGRETTE
PEAR TARTE TATIN

Chicken à la Niçoise

A MEDITERRANEAN RAGOUT

Serves 4

1 **4-pound chicken, cut into pieces**
2 **teaspoons thyme**
 Salt and pepper to taste
5 **tablespoons olive oil**
½ **cup chopped lean salt pork**
3 **onions, chopped**
2 **cloves garlic**
1 **14-ounce can tomatoes**
2 **bay leaves**
½ **cup dry red wine**
½ **cup oil-cured ripe olives**
½ **cup chopped parsley**

S eason chicken pieces with thyme, salt and pepper. Set aside.

❦ Heat olive oil in large stock pot. Add salt pork and chicken. Sauté 15 minutes, browning chicken pieces on all sides.

❦ Remove pork and chicken from pot, discarding pork. Add onions to stock pot and cook over low heat for 10 minutes, adding more oil if necessary. Add chicken, garlic, tomatoes, bay leaves and red wine. Mix well. Simmer uncovered, for 35 to 40 minutes, basting chicken frequently.

❦ Prior to serving, remove bay leaves and garlic. Add olives and sprinkle with parsley.

Chicken Breasts Ratatouille

SERVE THIS RUSTIC CASSEROLE WITH
A SALAD OF MIXED GREENS

Serves 4–6

¼ **cup olive oil**
½ **cup vegetable oil**
1 **clove garlic**
1 **onion, chopped**
½ **green pepper, chopped**
1 **eggplant, peeled and diced**
1 **zucchini, sliced**
2 **tomatoes, peeled and diced**
10 **mushrooms, sliced**
1 **6-ounce can tomato paste**
2 **cups water**
1 **teaspoon salt**
¼ **teaspoon dried basil**
¼ **teaspoon chervil**
 Pinch of rosemary
 Pinch of marjoram
4 **whole chicken breasts, halved, skinned and boned**
1¼ **cups chicken stock**
2 **tablespoons butter**

I n large skillet, heat ⅛ cup olive oil and ¼ cup vegetable oil. Sauté garlic, onion and green pepper until soft. Add remaining oils and sauté remaining vegetables for 15 minutes. Add tomato paste and water. Mix well. Add salt and herbs. Cover and simmer at least 1 hour. Ratatouille can be prepared in advance and kept in refrigerator for several days.

❦ In Dutch oven, combine chicken, stock and butter. Bring to a boil. Reduce to simmer and cook, covered, for 20 minutes. Serve topped with hot ratatouille.

Norwegian Stuffed Chicken

COLORFUL VEGETABLES AND CHEESE
FORM A CREAMY STUFFING

Serves 6

³/₄	**pound fresh spinach, stems removed, torn into small pieces**
1½	**cups shredded Jarlsberg cheese**
½	**cup fresh bread crumbs**
½	**cup shredded carrots**
½	**cup sliced scallions**
2	**tablespoons snipped fresh dill**
½	**teaspoon salt**
⅛	**teaspoon pepper**
1	**egg, well beaten**
¼	**cup plus 2 tablespoons chopped parsley**
3	**whole chicken breasts, split**
4	**tablespoons butter, melted**
2	**tablespoons lemon juice**

Combine spinach, cheese, bread crumbs, carrots, scallions, dill, salt, pepper, egg and ¼ cup chopped parsley in bowl. Stuff spinach mixture between breast meat and skin. Place chicken, skin side up, in shallow baking dish. Combine butter, lemon juice and remaining parsley. Drizzle over chicken.

❧ Bake at 375 degrees until tender, approximately 45 minutes. Baste frequently with pan drippings.

Chicken Florentine

CHICKEN ON A BED OF
CREAMY SPINACH

Serves 4

³/₄	**pound fresh spinach, stems removed**
½	**cup sour cream**
½	**cup mayonnaise**
1	**tablespoon finely chopped onion**
¼	**teaspoon nutmeg**
3	**tablespoons butter**
1	**teaspoon paprika**
½	**teaspoon sage**
½	**teaspoon thyme**
1	**clove garlic, crushed**
2	**whole chicken breasts, halved, skinned and boned**
2	**tablespoons lemon juice**
½	**teaspoon salt**
¼	**teaspoon pepper**

Steam spinach until wilted. Mix together sour cream, mayonnaise, onion and nutmeg. Add spinach. Spread mixture evenly over bottom of shallow baking dish.

❧ Melt butter in skillet over medium heat. Add seasonings and stir until hot and frothy, about 3 minutes. Add chicken and cook, turning once, until brown on both sides, about 5 minutes. Place chicken on top of spinach mixture. Pour skillet drippings over chicken and sprinkle with 1 tablespoon lemon juice, salt and pepper. Cover and bake at 325 degrees for 25 minutes, until fork can be inserted easily. Sprinkle with remaining lemon juice.

Chicken Breasts Veronique

ATTRACTIVE AND DELICATELY SEASONED

Serves 6

3	**whole chicken breasts, halved, skinned and boned**
1	**cup cracker crumbs**
½	**teaspoon salt**
¼	**teaspoon pepper**
¼	**teaspoon tarragon**
7	**tablespoons butter**
¼	**cup chopped shallots**
½	**cup chicken stock**
½	**cup dry white wine**
½	**pound fresh mushrooms, sliced**
2	**cups seedless green grapes**

Mix cracker crumbs with salt, pepper and tarragon. Lightly dredge chicken in mixture.

❧ Melt 4 tablespoons butter in skillet and brown chicken on both sides. Place pieces in single layer in shallow baking dish.

❧ Add shallots to skillet and sauté until translucent. Stir in stock and wine and bring to a boil. Pour over chicken. Bake at 375 degrees, uncovered, for 30 minutes.

❧ Sauté mushrooms in remaining 3 tablespoons butter. Add mushrooms and grapes to chicken. Bake an additional 8 to 10 minutes.

Honey Glazed Chicken

HONEY, CURRY AND COCONUT
ADD A SPECIAL TASTE

Serves 4–6

6   **tablespoons butter, melted**

⅓   **cup honey**

1   **tablespoon Dijon mustard**

1   **tablespoon curry powder**

3   **whole chicken breasts, halved, skinned and boned**

½   **cup shredded coconut**

Combine butter, honey, mustard and curry. Dip each chicken breast in mixture and place in shallow casserole. Bake at 325 degrees for 30 minutes, basting twice with honey-mustard mixture. Sprinkle chicken with coconut and bake an additional 15 minutes.

Germaine's Glazed Chicken

FROM CHEF GERMAINE SWANSON,
GERMAINE'S RESTAURANT

Serves 6

3   **egg whites, lightly beaten**

2   **cups plus 2 tablespoons vegetable oil**

4   **tablespoons cornstarch**

6   **chicken breast halves, boned, skinned and cut into 1″ strips**

1   **teaspoon minced garlic**

1   **teaspoon minced ginger**

5   **tablespoons soy sauce**

3   **tablespoons Chinese mushroom sauce (duck sauce may be substituted)**

2   **tablespoons Chinese black vinegar**

1   **tablespoon rice wine vinegar**

5   **tablespoons sugar**

1   **teaspoon chili paste with garlic**

1   **tablespoon toasted sesame seeds**

1   **large ripe tomato, sliced**

Combine egg whites, 2 tablespoons oil and 3 tablespoons cornstarch. Beat until smooth. Pour over chicken strips and marinate at room temperature for 20 minutes.

❧ Mix together garlic, ginger, soy sauce, mushroom sauce, vinegars, sugar and chili paste and set aside. In wok or frying pan, heat 2 cups oil over high heat. Add chicken strips in small batches and fry until crisp. Remove with slotted spoon and drain on paper towels.

❧ Dissolve remaining 1 tablespoon cornstarch in 2 tablespoons cold water. Pour all but 1 tablespoon oil from pan and add sauce mixture. Bring to a boil, add cornstarch and cook over low heat until thickened. Return chicken strips to pan and stir to coat pieces well.

❧ Arrange chicken on plate, sprinkle with sesame seeds and garnish with slices of tomato.

Marbella Chicken

PRUNES ADD AN UNEXPECTED FLAVOR

Serves 8

8–10 cloves garlic, crushed
¼ cup dried oregano
1 cup white wine
1 cup pitted prunes
½ cup capers with juice
1 cup light brown sugar
½ cup red wine vinegar
½ cup olive oil
½ cup pitted green olives
6 bay leaves
 Salt and pepper to taste
4 whole chicken breasts, halved, skinned and boned
¼ cup chopped parsley or cilantro

Mix together garlic, oregano, wine, prunes, capers, brown sugar, vinegar, oil, olives, bay leaves, salt and pepper.

❦ Arrange chicken in baking dish. Cover with marinade and refrigerate overnight. Bake at 350 degrees for 30 to 40 minutes. Prior to serving, drain remaining liquid and garnish with parsley.

Tandoori Chicken

THE YOGURT MARINADE GIVES
A SPICY FLAVOR

Serves 8

4 whole chicken breasts, halved, skinned and boned
2½ cups plain low-fat yogurt
3 tablespoons lemon juice
4 tablespoons olive oil
½ cup chopped onion
2″ piece ginger root, grated
6 cloves garlic, crushed
1 tablespoon cumin
1 tablespoon ground coriander
1 tablespoon cardamom
2 teaspoons salt
1 teaspoon turmeric
1 teaspoon cayenne pepper
½ teaspoon cinnamon
½ teaspoon black pepper
¼ teaspoon nutmeg
¼ teaspoon ground cloves
¼ teaspoon mace

Slash chicken breasts in 2 or 3 places. Process remaining ingredients in food processor. Marinate chicken in mixture at least 24 hours.

❦ Grill until done, approximately 20 minutes.

Poulet l'Oasis

APPLES AND ALMONDS GARNISH
THIS LOVELY DISH

Serves 4–6

3 chicken breasts, halved, skinned and boned
2 tablespoons butter
1 cup port or Madeira
1 cup beef stock
2 cups crème frâiche
 Salt and pepper to taste
3 apples, cored and peeled
½ cup slivered almonds, toasted

Sauté chicken breasts for 5 minutes in 1 tablespoon butter. Add port and stock and let stand in refrigerator at least 2 to 3 hours. Chicken may be prepared a day in advance up to this point.

❦ Remove chicken breasts from marinade. Add crème frâiche to marinade and boil, stirring, until sauce is syrupy and golden brown in color, approximately 20 minutes. Combine chicken with sauce. Season with salt and pepper. Cook gently for 15 minutes.

❦ Cut each apple into 8 slices. Sauté slices in remaining 1 tablespoon butter until tender. Set aside.

❦ Garnish chicken with apples and almonds.

Sherried Chicken Breasts

THIS FEATURES AN UNUSUAL
CURRY-LIKE SPICE

Serves 4

2   **tablespoons flour**
    Salt and pepper to taste
1   **clove garlic, crushed**
1   **teaspoon Guaram Masala**
2   **chicken breasts, halved and skinned**
½   **cup butter**
3   **tablespoons lemon juice**
3   **tablespoons soy sauce**
¾   **cup dry sherry**
½   **teaspoon ginger powder**

Mix flour, salt, pepper, garlic and Guaram Masala. Roll chicken in flour mixture and sauté in 2 tablespoons butter until browned on all sides. Remove chicken to baking pan and set aside.

In small saucepan, mix together remaining 6 tablespoons butter, lemon juice, soy sauce, sherry and ginger. Bring to a boil and simmer 15 minutes. Pour sauce over chicken breasts. Chicken may be refrigerated at this point to enhance flavors.

Bake at 350 degrees for 30 minutes, turning chicken once during baking.

Note: Guaram Masala is a spice available at gourmet shops.

Chicken Breasts Tarragon

A CREAMY BLEND OF FLAVORS

Serves 6–8

4   **whole chicken breasts, halved, skinned**
    and boned
2   **tablespoons olive oil**
4   **tablespoons butter**
6   **shallots, chopped**
2   **carrots, sliced**
¼   **cup cognac or brandy**
¾   **cup dry white wine**
¼   **cup chopped fresh tarragon**
    Salt and pepper to taste
1   **cup light cream**
1   **egg yolk**
1   **tablespoon flour**
¼   **pound mushrooms, sliced**

Sauté chicken in oil and 3 tablespoons butter until lightly browned on all sides. Remove from pan.

Add shallots and carrots to pan and sauté until tender. Return chicken to pan. Add brandy, white wine, tarragon, salt and pepper. Bring to a boil. Reduce heat, cover and simmer for 30 minutes.

Whisk together cream, egg yolk and flour. Remove chicken from pan and place on serving dish. Keep warm. Remove shallots and carrots from pan with slotted spoon and discard. Add cream mixture to pan drippings and heat almost to boiling, stirring constantly. Add additional wine if sauce becomes too thick.

Sauté mushrooms in remaining tablespoon of butter until just tender. Spoon sauce over chicken and garnish with mushrooms.

Sherried Artichoke Chicken

A MELLOW-FLAVORED CASSEROLE

Serves 8–10

- 6 **whole chicken breasts, halved, skinned and boned**
- 1 **tablespoon paprika**
- 2 **teaspoons salt**
- 1 **tablespoon pepper**
- ½ **cup butter**
- 2 **15-ounce cans artichoke hearts, drained and quartered**
- 1 **pound fresh mushrooms, sliced**
- ½ **teaspoon dried tarragon**
- 2 **rounded tablespoons flour**
- 1¼ **cups dry sherry**
- 2 **cups chicken stock**

Sprinkle chicken with paprika, salt and pepper. Sauté chicken in 6 tablespoons butter until browned. Place chicken in large casserole dish with artichoke hearts. Sauté mushrooms and tarragon in remaining 2 tablespoons butter for 5 minutes. Add flour and cook for 2 minutes. Add sherry and stock, whisking until blended. Simmer 5 minutes until sauce thickens.

❧ Pour sauce over chicken and cover casserole. Bake at 350 degrees for 30 to 40 minutes, adding more stock while baking if chicken becomes too dry.

Chicken Breasts in Sherried Tomato Cream

THE VELVETY SAUCE ADDS
A NICE FINISH

Serves 4

- 2 **whole chicken breasts, halved, skinned and boned**
- ½ **teaspoon salt**
- ½ **teaspoon white pepper**
- ½ **teaspoon nutmeg**
- 1½ **tablespoons butter**
- ¼ **cup finely chopped onion**
- ¼ **cup chopped parsley**
- ¼ **teaspoon dried basil**
- ⅓ **cup dry sherry**
- 1 **teaspoon Dijon mustard**
- 1 **medium tomato, peeled, seeded and chopped**
- ½ **cup heavy cream**

Sprinkle chicken breasts on both sides with salt, pepper and nutmeg. Sauté chicken in butter over medium-high heat until lightly browned. Add onions while browning second side.

❧ Add parsley, basil and sherry to chicken. As mixture comes to a boil, reduce heat, cover and simmer for approximately 20 minutes.

❧ Transfer chicken to serving dish, cover loosely and keep warm. Stir mustard into liquid in pan. Add tomato and cream. Bring to a boil. Cook and stir until liquid is slightly thickened.

❧ Spoon sauce over chicken and serve.

Southern Country Captain

A SAVORY SOUTHERN MEAL

Serves 6–8

1 4-pound chicken, cut into pieces
¾ cup butter
1 large onion, chopped
1 large green pepper, chopped
1 clove garlic, minced
1 8-ounce can tomatoes
1 cup chopped parsley
2 teaspoons vinegar
2 tablespoons prepared mustard
1 tablespoon Worcestershire sauce
1 tablespoon paprika
1 teaspoon curry powder
1 teaspoon thyme
1 teaspoon salt
1 teaspoon pepper
¼ pound fresh mushrooms, sliced
1 cup currants
¼ cup flour
½ cup slivered almonds

Bake or boil chicken until tender. Cool, remove skin and bones and cut chicken into bite-size pieces.

❧ Sauté onion, pepper and garlic in butter until soft, but not brown. Add remaining ingredients and blend. Add chicken pieces.

❧ Transfer to casserole dish and cover. Bake at 350 degrees for 1 hour.

Chicken Strudel

A CHEESY CHICKEN PASTRY

Serves 8–10

4 whole chicken breasts, halved
1 onion, halved
1 onion, chopped
2 tablespoons olive oil
2 cups chopped fresh spinach
2 cups grated Monterey Jack cheese
2 tablespoons dry white wine
¼ teaspoon salt
¼ teaspoon pepper
1 egg
10 sheets phyllo dough
½ cup butter, melted
⅔ cup dried bread crumbs
½ teaspoon paprika

Place chicken breasts in 3- to 4-quart saucepan. Add halved onion. Simmer in 2″ water until chicken is tender, approximately 35 minutes. When cooled, skin, debone, and cut chicken into ½″ pieces. Set aside.

❧ In skillet, sauté chopped onion in oil until tender. Add spinach and cook until wilted, about 3 minutes. Remove skillet from heat and stir in cheese, wine, salt, pepper, egg and chicken. Set aside.

❧ Place 1 sheet phyllo dough on waxed paper. Brush phyllo with melted butter and sprinkle with 1 tablespoon bread crumbs. Layer with 4 more sheets of phyllo, brushing each sheet with butter and sprinkling with bread crumbs. Spoon half of chicken mixture in 2″ strip along bottom 16″ length of phyllo. Roll phyllo jellyroll fashion. Repeat with remaining ingredients to make second roll.

❧ Place rolls, seam side down, on cookie sheet. Brush with remaining butter. With sharp knife, score diagonally to make 1″ slices. Sprinkle with paprika.

❧ Bake at 375 degrees for 15 to 20 minutes.

Chicken Piccata

LIGHT AND EASY

Serves 4–6

4 whole chicken breasts, halved, skinned and boned
   Salt and pepper to taste
1 tablespoon flour
2 tablespoons butter
2 tablespoons olive oil
1 pound mushrooms, sliced
½ cup dry white wine
¼ cup fresh lemon juice
3 tablespoons capers
4 teaspoons grated Parmesan cheese
¼ cup chopped fresh parsley

Pound chicken to ¼″ thickness. Sprinkle with salt, pepper and flour.

❦ Brown chicken on both sides in 1 tablespoon butter and 1 tablespoon olive oil. Remove to platter. Add remaining butter and olive oil to skillet and sauté mushrooms. Remove mushrooms with slotted spoon and set aside.

❦ Add white wine and lemon juice to mushroom juice in skillet. Deglaze pan and simmer a few minutes. Add capers and Parmesan. Return chicken and mushrooms to skillet and simmer 3 minutes. Turn and simmer 2 minutes more.

❦ If necessary, thicken pan juices with flour. Sprinkle with fresh parsley and garnish with thin lemon slices.

Chicken Crab Divan

A RICH MARRIAGE OF
CHICKEN AND CRAB

Serves 6–8

4 whole chicken breasts, halved, skinned and boned
7 tablespoons butter
8 ounces fresh crab meat
¼ cup dry sherry
   Salt and pepper to taste
½ cup quartered mushrooms
¼ cup finely chopped onion
3 tablespoons flour
1⅓ cups heavy cream
1 cup milk
½ cup chopped parsley
   Dash cayenne pepper
¼ cup grated Parmesan cheese
2 15-ounce cans artichoke hearts
   Paprika

In large skillet, cook chicken in 4 tablespoons butter 15 minutes. Add crab and cook another 5 minutes. Add sherry and allow to evaporate quickly. Season with salt and pepper. Remove chicken and crab and keep warm.

❦ Add remaining 3 tablespoons butter to pan drippings. Sauté mushrooms and onions. Stir in flour. Gradually add cream and milk, stirring constantly. Stir in parsley and cayenne pepper. Remove from heat. Blend in Parmesan cheese.

❦ Arrange drained artichoke hearts on bottom of greased 12″ × 8″ baking dish. Cover with half of sauce. Add chicken and crab and top with remaining sauce. Sprinkle with paprika. Bake uncovered at 375 degrees for 20 minutes.

Chicken with Mushrooms and Marsala

CHICKEN BREASTS POACHED IN A
CLASSIC WINE SAUCE

Serves 4

2   whole chicken breasts, halved, skinned
    and boned
1   cup flour
¼   teaspoon salt
¼   teaspoon white pepper
½   cup butter
2   cups sliced fresh mushrooms
1   cup Marsala wine
    Parsley for garnish

Pound chicken breasts to ¼″ thickness.
Coat chicken with mixture of flour, salt
and white pepper.

❦ Melt ¼ cup butter in skillet and sauté
mushrooms. Remove mushrooms, add
remaining butter and brown chicken on
both sides. Return mushrooms to skillet
and add wine. Simmer until chicken is
done and sauce thickens.

❦ Garnish with fresh parsley.

Cornish Hens with Wild Rice Stuffing

WILD RICE STUFFING CAN
BE PREPARED IN ADVANCE

Serves 4

4   Cornish game hens
½   lemon
½   teaspoon salt
½   teaspoon pepper
1   6-ounce box long grain and wild rice
1   chicken bouillon cube
2   tablespoons butter
¾   cup chopped mushrooms
¼   cup chopped onion
¼   cup chopped parsley
¼   cup baked ham, cut into thin strips
¼   cup slivered almonds
8   strips bacon

Rub cavity and skin of each hen with
lemon and sprinkle with salt and
pepper.

❦ Prepare rice according to package
directions, adding bouillon cube to water.
Sauté mushrooms and onion in butter
until tender. Stir in parsley, ham and
almonds. Cook 5 minutes. Combine
mushroom mixture with cooked rice.
Stuff hens with mixture.

❦ Place 2 strips bacon on top of each hen.
Bake at 350 degrees for 50 minutes.

Cornish Hens with Pistachio Raisin Stuffing

THIS STUFFING WOULD ALSO ENHANCE A
CROWN LAMB ROAST

Serves 4

½   cup golden raisins
¼   cup cognac
4   tablespoons butter
¼   cup chopped shallots
½   teaspoon salt
1½   cups cooked rice
¼   cup chopped pistachios
4   Cornish game hens

Bring raisins and cognac to a boil.
Remove from heat and let stand
10 minutes. Drain raisins.

❦ Sauté raisins and shallots in butter until
shallots are translucent. Stir in salt, rice
and pistachios.

❦ Fill cavity of each hen with stuffing.
Bake at 350 degrees for 1 hour.

Drunk Duck

GRAND MARNIER MAKES
THE DIFFERENCE

Serves 2–4

- 1 3–5 pound duck
- 1 apple, peeled and sliced
- 2 stalks celery
- 1 onion

Orange Sauce:

- ½ cup sugar
- 1 tablespoon red wine vinegar
- 2 oranges
- ¼ cup Grand Marnier
- 1 lemon
- 1–2 tablespoons arrowroot

Stuff cavity of duck with apple, celery and onion. Place on rack in roasting pan. Place duck in 450 degree oven and immediately reduce heat to 350 degrees. Roast until done, allowing 20 to 30 minutes per pound. Prick duck often to allow excess fat to escape.

For orange sauce, cook sugar and vinegar until sugar caramelizes, stirring constantly. Remove from heat. Add juice of 2 oranges, Grand Marnier and grated rind of 1 orange. Return to stove and simmer until all caramel is dissolved. Add duck juices and bring to a boil. Add lemon juice. Cut peel of half of remaining orange and whole lemon into very thin strips. Add to sauce. If necessary, thicken with 1 to 2 tablespoons arrowroot.

Before serving, remove fat from duck and glaze with orange sauce.

Julienne of Roasted Duck in Currant Cumberland Vinaigrette

FROM RIDGEWELL'S CATERERS

Serves 8

- 1 5-pound duck
- 1 tablespoon tumeric powder
- Salt and pepper to taste
- ½ pound shiitake mushrooms, cut into ⅛" strips
- 1 celery stalk, cut into ⅛" thick diagonal slices
- ½ cup chopped pecans

Currant Cumberland Vinaigrette:

- ¼ cup red currant jelly
- ⅛ cup ruby port wine
- Juice and grated rind of 1 lemon
- 2 garlic cloves, minced
- 1 shallot, chopped
- 1 teaspoon cayenne pepper
- 1 teaspoon ginger
- ½ cup vegetable oil

Prick duck all over with trussing needle or skewer. Rub with tumeric, salt and pepper. Place on rack in roasting pan. Roast at 375 degrees for 2 hours. When cool, refrigerate.

For vinaigrette, stir jelly and port wine together until smooth. Add juice and rind. Stir in remaining ingredients. Set aside.

Pull off skin and remove duck meat from bones. Cut into slivers. In skillet, combine duck meat, mushrooms, celery and vinaigrette. Cover and cook for 30 minutes, stirring occasionally. Spoon into serving dish and sprinkle with pecans.

Crispy Duck Szechuan

FROM CHEF BOON LIM,
CHINA REGENCY

Serves 2–4

- 1 duck
- ½ cup white wine
- Salt and pepper to taste
- 5 scallions, cut in 3" lengths
- Ginger root, cut in 2" strips and crushed
- Peanut oil

Rub duck inside and out with wine and sprinkle with salt and pepper. Stuff cavity with half the scallions and ginger and place remaining on top. Refrigerate overnight.

Steam duck until tender, approximately 1 to 2 hours. Remove ginger and scallions.

Cut duck into serving-size pieces. Cook in oil until skin is brown and crispy.

PASTA, RICE & VEGETABLES

Pasta Shells al Gorgonzola

GORGONZOLA INFUSES A PUNGENT FLAVOR

Serves 4–6

½ cup butter
¼ pound Gorgonzola cheese
1 cup half-and-half
2 tablespoons cognac
3 tablespoons tomato purée
⅔ cup shelled pistachios, coarsely chopped
1 pound small pasta shells
2 cups grated Parmesan cheese
½ cup finely chopped fresh basil

Melt butter in skillet and add Gorgonzola, stirring until smooth. Add half-and-half, cognac, tomato purée and nuts.

❧ Cook pasta shells in boiling water until just tender. Drain and toss with sauce and 1 cup Parmesan cheese. Garnish with chopped basil. Serve remaining Parmesan cheese on side.

Pasta Tricolore

BEAUTIFUL YET SIMPLE

Serves 4–6

1 red pepper, julienned
1 yellow pepper, julienned
3 shallots, finely chopped
⅓ cup butter
1 pound fresh spinach pasta
1 cup milk
½ cup heavy cream
3 tablespoons sherry
2 tablespoons tomato paste
1 cup grated Parmesan cheese
¼ cup toasted pine nuts

Sauté peppers and shallots in butter.

❧ Cook pasta al dente. In small saucepan, combine milk, cream, sherry and tomato paste and simmer for 2 to 3 minutes. Toss with cooked pasta and pepper mixture.

❧ Sprinkle Parmesan cheese and pine nuts over pasta before serving.

Creamy Lemon Chive
Pasta with Asparagus

A REFRESHING SPRING DISH

Serves 4 as an appetizer, 2 as a main course

½ **pound fettucine**

½ **pound fresh asparagus, trimmed and cut into ½" pieces**

2 **tablespoons butter, melted**

2 **egg yolks**

1 **cup heavy cream**

½ **cup grated Parmesan cheese**

1 **tablespoon chives**

1 **teaspoon grated lemon rind**

Salt and pepper to taste

1 **slice of lemon, quartered**

Cook fettucine al dente and drain. Cook asparagus until just tender, about 3 to 4 minutes. Drain and add to pasta. Toss fettucine and asparagus with melted butter and set aside.

❦ Whisk egg yolks in small bowl, then add cream and Parmesan cheese. Add cream mixture to pasta, toss and heat through over low heat until Parmesan cheese is melted. Stir in chives, lemon rind, salt and pepper.

❦ Divide pasta among plates and garnish with lemon quarters and additional chives, if desired.

Fettucine with Basil,
Green Beans and Walnuts

THIS DISH NEEDS ONLY A GLASS OF
WINE AND CRUSTY BREAD

Serves 2–4

½ **cup chopped walnuts**

3 **tablespoons butter**

2–3 **shallots, finely chopped**

¾ **cup fresh basil leaves, julienned**

2 **large garlic cloves, minced**

1 **cup chicken stock or water**

1 **cup crème fraîche**

Salt and pepper to taste

¾ **pound small green beans**

¾ **pound fresh fettucine**

Grated lemon rind for garnish

4–5 **whole basil leaves for garnish**

Grated Parmesan cheese for garnish

Toast walnuts in oven for 5 to 7 minutes. Melt butter in large saucepan and add shallots, cooking over medium heat for 1 minute. Add 2 tablespoons basil, garlic and stock or water. Cook over medium heat until shallots are softened. Stir in crème fraîche and cook until slightly thickened. Season with salt and pepper.

❦ Bring large pot of salted water to boil. Add green beans and cook for 2 to 3 minutes. Remove beans with a slotted spoon, reserving water. Add beans to cream and shallot mixture.

❦ In reserved water, cook pasta al dente. Drain well and add to beans with remaining basil. Toss lightly. Add walnuts and toss once more. Garnish with grated lemon rind, a few whole basil leaves and Parmesan cheese.

Saffron Cream Pasta

GREEN VEGETABLES MAKE A STRIKING
CONTRAST TO THE SAFFRON CREAM

Serves 4

1/4 teaspoon saffron
2 tablespoons boiling water
1 pound asparagus, trimmed
1 pound fresh pasta
1 tablespoon unsalted butter
2 shallots, finely chopped
1½ cups light cream
  Salt and pepper to taste
1 10-ounce package frozen peas, thawed
1 strip lemon peel, finely sliced
  Fresh Parmesan cheese

Immerse saffron in boiling water. Set aside.

❦ Cut off asparagus tips into 2″ lengths. Cut remaining stalks diagonally into bite-size pieces. Cook asparagus in boiling salted water until tender. Remove with slotted spoon and set aside. In the same pot, cook pasta al dente.

❦ While pasta is cooking, melt butter in skillet and gently cook shallots until they are soft, approximately 5 to 7 minutes. Add cream and saffron water. Boil to reduce slightly and season with salt and pepper. Add asparagus and peas. When pasta is done, add to cream sauce, turning to coat. Add lemon peel and serve immediately topped with Parmesan cheese.

Pasta Milano

MOZZARELLA GIVES BODY TO THIS
PASTA DISH

Serves 4

1 pound fresh pappardelle or other small, shaped pasta
1 teaspoon butter
1 tablespoon heavy cream
3½ ounces mozzarella cheese, shredded
1 cup tomato sauce (recipe below)
  Grated Parmesan cheese to taste
1/4 cup chopped fresh basil plus extra for garnish
  Pepper to taste

Cook pasta al dente in boiling salted water. Drain. Combine butter, cream, mozzarella and tomato sauce in large skillet. Cook over low heat. Add pasta to skillet. Stir 1 minute. Before serving, add Parmesan cheese, basil and pepper. Garnish with additional basil.

Tomato Sauce:
Yields 1½ cups

3 tablespoons olive oil
1 tablespoon minced garlic
2 cups crushed tomatoes
1 teaspoon oregano
1/2 teaspoon dried rosemary
  Salt and pepper to taste
2 tablespoons finely chopped fresh basil or 1 teaspoon dried basil

Heat oil in saucepan. Add garlic and cook briefly, stirring constantly. Add tomatoes, oregano, rosemary, salt and pepper. Bring to a boil, reduce heat and cook for 15 minutes, stirring occasionally. Stir in basil.

Spinach Pasta with Salmon

BALANCE THIS LUXURIOUS DISH
WITH A CRISP SALAD

Serves 4

½ **pound salmon fillet**
2 **cups dry white wine**
4 **sprigs parsley**
5-6 **black peppercorns**
2 **cups heavy cream**
    Pinch of nutmeg
4 **tablespoons unsalted butter, melted**
1 **teaspoon salt**
1 **pound fresh spinach linguine**
2 **tablespoons grated Parmesan cheese**
½ **cup chopped fresh dill**

Poach salmon in wine, parsley and peppercorns for 10 minutes. Cool, then flake salmon with fork, removing skin and bones.

❧ Simmer cream, nutmeg, salt and 2 tablespoons of butter in saucepan until cream is reduced by one-third.

❧ Cook linguine al dente in boiling salted water, approximately 3 to 5 minutes. While pasta is cooking, stir Parmesan cheese, salmon and ¼ cup of fresh dill into cream mixture.

❧ Toss drained linguine with remaining 2 tablespoons butter and divide pasta onto plates. Spoon salmon cream sauce over linguine and garnish with remaining fresh dill.

Ravioli aux Betteraves Rouge et Caviar

FROM CHEF YANNICK CAM,
LE PAVILLON

Serves 4

Beet Purée:

1 **pound red beets**
¼ **onion, thinly sliced**
1 **tablespoon butter**
1 **teaspoon salt**

Simmer beets until tender, approximately 2 hours. Purée in food processor or blender. Place purée in saucepan and cook over low heat until purée is reduced to thick paste, approximately 6 to 8 minutes.

❧ Sauté onion slices in butter until tender, approximately 2 to 3 minutes. Purée in food processor or blender. Place in saucepan and cook over low heat until purée thickens.

❧ Combine purées and add salt. Cool.

Ravioli:

1 **cup high gluten flour**
1 **egg**
1 **teaspoon olive oil**
   Chive Butter Sauce
1 **medium tomato, peeled, seeded and finely diced**
   Osetra caviar

In food processor fitted with steel blade, process flour, egg, olive oil and ¼ cup beet purée until fairly dry. Remove from food processor and knead by hand for several minutes. Wrap in plastic wrap and set aside for 1 hour. Pasta will become pliable while resting.

❧ Using pasta machine, roll out pasta until quite thin. Pass through pasta machine twice to finish. Cut strips of pasta into manageable lengths. Using a cookie cutter, cut pasta into circles. Place ½ teaspoon beet purée on 1 side of each circle and fold over to form crescent. Press lightly to seal.

❧ Drop ravioli into simmering water. Cook approximately 1 minute. Drain.

❧ Pipe or spoon Chive Butter Sauce onto individual plates and arrange 5 to 7 ravioli in circle on each. Place small amount of diced tomato on the side and top each ravioli with ⅛ teaspoon osetra caviar. Serve immediately.

Chive Butter Sauce:

1 **tablespoon finely minced chives**
½ **cup butter, at room temperature**

Whirl chives and butter in food processor.

Rigate
with Yellow Pear Tomatoes
and Tarragon Cream

SAUTEED TOMATOES LEND A SPECIAL
SWEETNESS TO THE SAUCE

Serves 2

½–¾ **pound yellow pear tomatoes**

1 **tablespoon unsalted butter**

1 **cup light cream**

1 **shallot, finely chopped**

1½ **tablespoons finely chopped fresh tarragon**

2 **tablespoons chopped parsley**

Salt and pepper to taste

½ **pound fresh rigate or other small, shell-shaped pasta**

¼ **cup grated Parmesan cheese**

Sauté tomatoes in butter and set aside. Heat cream with chopped shallot in skillet and bring to a slow boil. When sauce begins to thicken, add sautéed tomatoes and half the tarragon and parsley. Reduce to desired thickness, and season with salt and pepper.

❧ In boiling salted water, cook pasta al dente. Drain, then toss with tomato cream mixture and remaining tarragon and parsley. Sprinkle with Parmesan cheese.

Linguine all'Aragosta

FROM CHEF GIULIO SANTILLO,
RISTORANTE TIBERIO

Serves 4

4 **cloves garlic, minced**

2 **cups Italian olive oil**

2 **cans peeled Italian tomatoes**

4 **fresh basil leaves (optional)**

Salt and pepper to taste

4 **1½-pound lobsters**

2 **pinches crushed red pepper**

1 **pound thin linguine**

Lightly sauté 1 clove minced garlic in 1 cup oil. Add tomatoes, basil and ½ teaspoon salt and bring to a boil. Cook over medium heat for 30 minutes. Crush tomatoes with a whisk.

❧ While tomato sauce is cooking, prepare lobsters. Using a sharp, heavy knife, remove lobster claws. Discard legs. Split body in half by pressing the lobster stomach down, placing knife tip between head and body and splitting all the way to tail. Turn lobster around and split down the head in the same manner.

❧ In large frying pan, heat remaining 1 cup oil. Add remaining 3 cloves garlic and red pepper. Place claws and lobster in pan, meat side down. Cover and cook on high heat, approximately 4 minutes. Remove claws and cool. Break open to extract meat and return to pan.

❧ Add tomato sauce to frying pan; bring to a boil and cook over medium heat for 15 minutes.

❧ Cook pasta for 7 minutes. Drain. Toss with lobster sauce and serve immediately.

Pecan Pilaf

TO ACCOMPANY CORNISH HENS OR
A CROWN LAMB ROAST

Serves 6–8

6	tablespoons butter
1	cup chopped pecans
½	cup chopped onion
2	cups uncooked rice
2	cups chicken stock
2	cups water
½	teaspoon thyme
	Pepper to taste
3	tablespoons chopped fresh parsley

Melt 3 tablespoons butter in skillet over medium-high heat. Add pecans and sauté until lightly browned, about 2 to 3 minutes. Transfer pecans to small bowl and set aside.

❧ Melt remaining butter in same skillet. Add onions and sauté until tender. Stir in rice, coating well with butter.

❧ In a saucepan, bring stock, water, thyme, pepper and 2 tablespoons parsley to a boil. Add mixture to rice. Cover and simmer until liquid is absorbed, approximately 20 minutes. Add pecans and remaining parsley and fluff with fork.

Thai Fried Rice

A SPICY MELANGE OF RICE,
FRUIT AND VEGETABLES

Serves 10

1½	cups uncooked long-grain rice
2	tablespoons vegetable oil
1	tablespoon minced fresh ginger
¼	cup raisins
⅓	cup slivered toasted almonds
1	cup seeded and diced tomatoes
½	cup minced scallions
½	cup diced fresh pineapple
2	tablespoons lime juice

Sauce:

2¼	cups chicken stock
¼	cup unsweetened coconut milk
2	tablespoons light soy sauce
1	tablespoon lime juice
1	tablespoon curry powder
½	teaspoon Chinese chili sauce
½	teaspoon salt
½	teaspoon grated lemon peel

Combine sauce ingredients until well blended. Set aside.

❧ Rinse and drain rice. Heat oil over medium heat. Add ginger and sauté a few seconds. Stir in rice, coating well with oil. Heat 5 minutes. Stir in raisins and sauce and bring to a low boil. Cover and reduce heat. Simmer until liquid is absorbed, approximately 20 minutes. Stir in almonds, tomatoes, scallions, pineapple and lime juice

Apple-Walnut Rice

A CRUNCHY AUTUMN PILAF

Serves 6

1	6-ounce package long-grain and wild rice
⅓	cup Madeira
2	tablespoons butter
2	medium tart cooking apples, peeled and coarsely chopped
2	tablespoons brown sugar
1	cup sliced celery
½	cup chopped walnuts
¼	cup diced candied citron

Cook rice according to package directions, using Madeira as part of liquid.

❧ Melt butter in saucepan, add chopped apples and sprinkle with brown sugar. Cook until apples are tender but still hold their shape, stirring frequently.

❧ Stir apple mixture, celery, walnuts and citron into hot cooked rice. Heat through.

Rice Indienne

CURRIED RICE WITH A SWEET TOPPING

Serves 4

- 3 tablespoons butter
- 2 teaspoons curry
- 1 cup uncooked rice
- 2 cups chicken stock
- ⅔ cup seedless raisins
- ⅓ cup chopped scallions
- ⅓ cup chopped green pepper
- ⅓ cup chopped celery
- 2 tablespoons chutney
- 2 tablespoons chopped pimento
- 2 tablespoons chopped almonds
- 1 tablespoon cider vinegar
- 1 tablespoon brown sugar
- ½ teaspoon salt

In saucepan, combine 2 tablespoons butter, curry and rice. Cook over low heat for 5 minutes, stirring occasionally. Add chicken stock and heat to boiling. Stir, cover and cook over low heat until liquid is absorbed, about 15 minutes.

❧ While rice is cooking, combine raisins, scallions, green pepper, celery and remaining tablespoon of butter in saucepan and cook over low heat until vegetables are just tender. Add chutney, pimento, almonds, vinegar, brown sugar and salt to the vegetable mixture. Stir until well blended. Place rice on serving platter and spoon vegetable mixture over top.

Pebble Garden, Dumbarton Oaks

AL FRESCO LUNCHEON

SHERRIED PEACH SOUP
HERBED PORK ROAST
CREAMY LEMON CHIVE PASTA WITH ASPARAGUS
SNOW PEA SALAD
BAVARIAN APPLE TORTE

Vermouth Asparagus

VERMOUTH AND PARMESAN MAKE
A PIQUANT DRESSING

Serves 4–6

1–1½ **pounds fresh asparagus, trimmed**
½ **cup butter**
¼ **cup dry vermouth**
2 **tablespoons lemon juice**
2 **tablespoons chopped parsley**
3 **tablespoons Parmesan cheese**
1 **teaspoon paprika**

Steam asparagus to desired tenderness.

❧ Melt butter in small saucepan. Stir in vermouth, lemon juice and parsley. Heat through and pour over cooked asparagus. Sprinkle with Parmesan cheese and paprika.

Asparagus with Orange-Buttered Crumbs

ORANGE CRUMBS IMPART
COLOR AND ZEST

Serves 6

2 **pounds fresh asparagus, trimmed**
½ **cup butter**
1 **cup fine, dry bread crumbs**
2 **teaspoons grated orange rind**
　　Orange slices for garnish

Cook asparagus in boiling water until just tender, approximately 6 to 8 minutes. Drain thoroughly.

❧ While asparagus is cooking, melt butter in skillet. Add bread crumbs. Cook over medium heat until crisp and golden brown. Remove from heat and stir in orange rind.

❧ Spoon crumbs over cooked asparagus and garnish with orange slices.

Dillicious Green Beans

A WARM VEGETABLE SALAD

Serves 6

1¼ **pounds fresh green beans, trimmed**
6 **tablespoons butter**
2 **tablespoons lemon juice**
1⅓ **teaspoons dried dill**
½ **clove garlic, crushed**
1 **tablespoon chopped parsley**
10 **cherry tomatoes, halved**
½ **cup sliced ripe olives**
　　Salt and pepper to taste

Cook beans in boiling salted water until just tender. Drain.

❧ Melt butter in pan. Add beans, lemon juice, dill, garlic and parsley. Toss over low heat.

❧ Add tomatoes and olives and heat through. Season with salt and pepper.

Marmalade Carrots

AN INNOVATIVE WAY TO SERVE CARROTS

Serves 6

2 **pounds carrots, julienned**
¼ **cup plus 2 tablespoons orange juice**
¼ **cup maple syrup**
2 **tablespoons orange marmalade**

S team carrots until just tender. Drain and set aside.

❧ Combine orange juice, maple syrup and marmalade in saucepan. Bring mixture to a boil, stirring constantly. Add carrots and stir to coat. Reduce heat and simmer for 3 minutes.

Carrot Pudding

A SWEET ACCOMPANIMENT TO ANY ROAST

Serves 6

2 **cups cooked, puréed carrots**
1 **cup sugar**
¼ **cup butter**
1 **cup milk**
2 **heaping tablespoons flour**
¼ **teaspoon cinnamon**
3 **eggs, slightly beaten**
1 **teaspoon baking powder**
   Pinch of salt

C ombine all ingredients. Bake in buttered casserole at 350 degrees until set, approximately 1½ hours.

Lemon-Glazed Carrots

A LUSCIOUS, LIGHT DISH

Serves 4

1 **pound carrots, peeled**
2 **tablespoons butter**
   Juice and grated rind of ½ lemon
2 **tablespoons sugar**
   Salt and pepper to taste

Q uarter and slice carrots lengthwise into 2″ strips. Cook carrots for 8 to 10 minutes in boiling water until tender. Drain.

❧ Combine butter, lemon juice and rind.

❧ Sauté carrots with lemon butter. Sprinkle with sugar, salt and pepper. Cook over high heat until glazed.

Cauliflower Bake

A WINTER VEGETABLE MELANGE

Serves 8

1 head cauliflower
1 16-ounce can tomatoes, undrained
1 medium onion, finely chopped
1 tablespoon diced green pepper
1 tablespoon sugar
1 teaspoon salt
¼ teaspoon pepper
¼ cup butter
½ cup grated cheddar cheese
¾ cup crackers or dry bread crumbs

Cook cauliflower in salted water for 10 minutes. Drain and break into pieces. Mix cauliflower, tomatoes, onion, green pepper, sugar, salt, pepper and butter. Transfer mixture to casserole dish and sprinkle cheese over top. Sprinkle with crumbs. Bake at 350 degrees until most of liquid is evaporated, approximately 40 minutes.

Scalloped Corn and Tomatoes

A FLAVORFUL MIX OF FAVORITE VEGETABLES

Serves 8–10

1 cup thinly sliced onion
6 tablespoons butter
2 pounds tomatoes, peeled and chopped
2 teaspoons sugar
2 teaspoons salt
1 teaspoon dried marjoram leaves
¼ teaspoon pepper
2 10-ounce packages frozen shoepeg corn, thawed
2 cups fresh bread crumbs
2 teaspoons chopped parsley

Sauté onion in 4 tablespoons butter until tender and golden, approximately 5 minutes. Stir in tomatoes, sugar, salt, marjoram, pepper and corn. Pour mixure into a 2-quart casserole.

❧ Melt remaining 2 tablespoons butter and stir in bread crumbs and parsley. Sprinkle over corn mixture. Bake uncovered at 350 degrees for 30 minutes or until browned.

Gratin of Kohlrabi and Bermuda Onions

FROM CHEF DOUGLAS MCNEILL, THE FOUR SEASONS HOTEL

Serves 6

1½ pounds kohlrabi, woody stem removed
1 large Bermuda onion
1 tablespoon corn oil
½ teaspoon salt
½ teaspoon cracked black pepper
   Pinch of cayenne
3 tablespoons white wine
1 cup heavy cream
½ clove garlic, crushed

Peel and thinly slice kohlrabi and Bermuda onion. Place in Dutch oven with oil. Sauté over medium heat, approximately 5 to 10 minutes. Add salt, pepper and cayenne. Add white wine and reduce until nearly dry. Add cream and simmer for 12 minutes.

❧ Rub gratin dish with garlic. Fill with kohlrabi and onion mixture and bake at 375 degrees for 15 minutes, or until golden brown.

Garlic Roasted Potatoes

RUSTIC AND SATISFYING

Serves 2

4 large new potatoes, quartered
4 tablespoons unsalted butter
    Salt and pepper to taste
6 cloves garlic

Melt butter in a skillet. Add potatoes and coat with butter on all sides. Season with salt and pepper. Cover skillet and cook over medium heat for 20 to 25 minutes, stirring occasionally.

❦ Add garlic cloves and cook an additional 5 to 10 minutes.

Basque Potatoes

A MEDITERRANEAN-STYLE DISH

Serves 6

3 pounds baking potatoes, peeled and sliced
6 tomatoes, quartered and seeded
8 slices bacon, cooked and crumbled
5 cloves garlic, minced
2 teaspoons fresh thyme or 3/4 teaspoon dried thyme
2 cups sliced mushrooms
1½ cups pitted ripe olives, quartered
    Salt and pepper to taste
½ cup dry sherry
½ cup butter, melted

Layer potatoes alternately with tomatoes in large, shallow baking dish. Sprinkle with bacon, 3 cloves minced garlic, thyme, mushrooms and olives. Season with salt and pepper. Pour sherry over potatoes. Cover and bake at 350 degrees for 30 minutes.

❦ Combine butter and remaining 2 cloves garlic. Pour over potatoes. Bake uncovered until potatoes are tender, approximately 40 to 45 minutes.

Coconut Sweet Potato Bake

COCONUT ADDS A NEW FLAVOR

Serves 8

4 cups hot mashed sweet potatoes
6 tablespoons butter, melted
1/3 cup plus 2 tablespoons brown sugar
2 eggs, beaten
½ cup milk
½ cup chopped pecans
½ cup flaked coconut
2 tablespoons flour

Combine sweet potatoes, 4 tablespoons butter and 2 tablespoons brown sugar. Beat in eggs and milk. Place mixture in a shallow, buttered casserole.

❦ Combine remaining brown sugar, pecans, coconut and flour. Stir in remaining melted butter. Sprinkle mixture over sweet potatoes.

❦ Bake at 325 degrees for 45 minutes.

Sweet Potato-Apple Scallop

LACED WITH APPLE PIE SPICES

Serves 6–8

6　large sweet potatoes
6　tart apples, peeled
1　cup butter, melted
1　cup brown sugar
¼　cup maple syrup
2　tablespoons cinnamon
½　teaspoon ground cloves
½　teaspoon ginger
½　teaspoon nutmeg

Boil sweet potatoes until just tender. Peel and slice into ½″ rounds. Core apples and slice into ½″ rounds. Layer sweet potatoes and apples in a buttered casserole.

❧　Combine butter, brown sugar, maple syrup and spices. Spoon over potatoes and apples. Bake uncovered at 350 degrees for approximately 1 hour.

Sweet Potato Soufflé

A SOPHISTICATED PRESENTATION FOR THIS FAVORITE WINTER VEGETABLE

Serves 6–8

2　cups cooked mashed sweet potatoes
　　Pinch of salt
½　cup sugar
¼　teaspoon mace
¼　teaspoon cinnamon
1　tablespoon grated orange peel
1　cup light cream
6　egg whites, at room temperature

Beat together sweet potatoes, salt, ¼ cup sugar, mace, cinnamon and orange peel. In small saucepan, scald cream. Add to sweet potato mixture and beat until smooth.

❧　Beat egg whites until soft peaks form. Gradually add remaining ¼ cup sugar and beat until stiff.

❧　Fold sweet potato mixture into egg whites. Gently spoon into a 6-cup soufflé dish. Bake in lower third of oven at 350 degrees until puffy and golden, approximately 45 minutes.

Sautéed Cherry Tomatoes

AN EASY, COLORFUL VEGETABLE DISH

Serves 6–8

8　tablespoons unsalted butter
3　pints cherry tomatoes
2　tablespoons sugar
　　Salt and pepper to taste
　　Parsley or dill for garnish

Melt butter in heavy skillet. Roll tomatoes in butter over high heat. Sprinkle with sugar, salt and pepper. Cook until shiny and heated through. Do not overcook or tomatoes will burst. Remove immediately and serve warm, garnished with parsley or dill.

Tomatoes Provençale

HOME-GROWN TOMATOES MAKE
THIS A TASTY DISH

Serves 6

3 medium tomatoes
¼ teaspoon salt
¼ teaspoon pepper
½ clove garlic, minced
3 tablespoons minced scallions
4 tablespoons minced parsley
⅛ teaspoon thyme
¼ cup olive oil
½ cup bread crumbs

Cut tomatoes in half crosswise. Gently press out juice and seeds. Sprinkle with salt and pepper.

❧ Blend remaining ingredients and spread evenly on tomatoes. Place tomatoes in roasting pan. Bake at 400 degrees for 10 to 15 minutes or until tomatoes are just tender.

Spinach Timbales

A DELICIOUS WAY TO ADD COLOR
TO A MEAL

Serves 8

½ cup chicken stock
1 cup heavy cream
1½ cups chopped, cooked spinach, squeezed dry
2 ounces Boursin cheese
5 eggs
½ teaspoon dry mustard
½ teaspoon Worcestershire sauce
  Dash of Tabasco
4 tablespoons grated Parmesan cheese
3 tablespoons chopped chives
8 whole spinach leaves plus additional for garnish
1 tablespoon unsalted butter, softened

Combine stock and cream. Place spinach, Boursin and 4 tablespoons stock mixture in blender or food processor and purée.

❧ Whisk together eggs, mustard, Worcestershire sauce, Tabasco and remaining stock mixture. Fold in spinach mixture, Parmesan cheese and chives. Blend thoroughly.

❧ Remove stems from spinach leaves and steam leaves until wilted. Butter 8 4-ounce timbale molds. Line each mold with a spinach leaf and fill three-quarters full with spinach mixture. Place timbales in pan high enough to be even with tops of molds. Fill pan with hot water to reach halfway up sides of molds. Bake at 350 degrees for 45 minutes.

❧ Remove molds from pan and let cool for 5 minutes. Invert onto platter or individual plates and garnish with whole spinach leaves.

Creamy Spinach Casserole

A MAKE-AHEAD DISH, PERFECT FOR BUFFETS

Serves 8–10

4 pounds fresh spinach or 5 packages frozen spinach, thawed
1 cup chopped onion
2 cloves garlic, minced
1/4 cup butter
1 cup heavy cream
1 cup milk
1/2 cup grated Parmesan cheese
1/2 cup plain bread crumbs
1 teaspoon marjoram
1 teaspoon salt
1 teaspoon pepper
1/4 cup grated sharp cheddar cheese

Trim fresh spinach and steam until just wilted. Press excess moisture from spinach. Sauté onion and garlic in butter until translucent.

❧ Combine all ingredients except cheddar cheese. Spoon into buttered casserole. Sprinkle top with cheddar cheese. Casserole may be refrigerated for several hours before baking.

❧ Bake at 350 degrees for 30 minutes.

Garden Stuffed Yellow Squash

A TASTEFUL PRESENTATION OF
THIS PLENTIFUL VEGETABLE

Serves 12

6 medium yellow squash
1 cup chopped onions
1 cup chopped tomatoes
1/2 cup chopped green pepper
1/2 cup shredded cheddar cheese
6 slices bacon, cooked and crumbled
Salt and pepper to taste
4 tablespoons butter

In large pot, cover squash with water and bring to a boil. Reduce heat. Cover and simmer until squash are tender but firm, approximately 8 to 10 minutes.

❧ Drain squash and cool slightly. Trim stems. Cut squash in half lengthwise. Remove pulp and chop. Reserve shells.

❧ Combine pulp with onions, tomatoes, green pepper, cheese and bacon. Place squash shells in 9″ × 13″ baking dish. Spoon vegetable mixture into shells. Dot with butter. Squash can be assembled to this point and refrigerated until baking time. Bake at 400 degrees for 20 to 25 minutes.

Spicy Squash Sauté

THIS WILL BECOME A FAVORITE SIDE DISH

Serves 4–6

1/4 cup butter
1 1/2 pounds zucchini or yellow squash, thinly sliced
1 medium yellow onion, thinly sliced
1 clove garlic, crushed
1/2 cup chopped scallions
1/2 teaspoon pepper
1/4 cup vegetable juice
1 teaspoon sugar

Melt butter in skillet over low heat. Add squash, yellow onion and garlic. Sauté 5 minutes, stirring often.

❧ Add scallions, pepper, vegetable juice and sugar, mixing well. Cover and simmer over low heat, stirring occasionally, until just tender, approximately 5 minutes.

Zucchini Imperial

SERVE AS A VEGETARIAN ENTREE

Serves 6–8

2 eggs, slightly beaten
1 cup mayonnaise
1 onion, chopped
¼ cup chopped green pepper
1 cup grated Parmesan cheese
   Salt and pepper to taste
4 cups sliced, cooked zucchini
1 tablespoon butter
2 tablespoons bread crumbs

Combine eggs, mayonnaise, onion, green pepper, cheese, salt and pepper. Stir in zucchini. Pour into shallow baking dish. Dot with butter and sprinkle with bread crumbs.

❦ Bake at 350 degrees for 30 minutes.

Zucchini Sausage Casserole

A CRUSTLESS QUICHE

Serves 12

2 pounds zucchini, ends trimmed
¼ cup chopped onion
1 pound hot or sweet sausage
½ cup fine cracker crumbs
2 eggs, slightly beaten
½ cup grated Parmesan cheese
   Pinch each of thyme, rosemary and garlic powder
   Salt and pepper to taste

Cook whole zucchini in boiling salted water until just tender, 10 to 15 minutes. Drain and chop coarsely.

❦ Brown onion and sausage in large skillet. Drain off fat. Add zucchini and remaining ingredients, except 2 tablespoons Parmesan cheese. Mix well. Divide mixture between 2 8″ pie plates. Sprinkle with reserved Parmesan cheese. Casseroles may be wrapped and frozen at this point, until ready to bake.

❦ Bake at 350 degrees for 45 minutes, or until firm and brown.

Zucchini Sauté

A LIGHT DISH WITH A HINT OF DILL

Serves 4

4 medium zucchini, grated
¾ teaspoon salt
4 tablespoons butter
3 scallions, chopped
1 tablespoon lemon juice
¼ teaspoon dill
   Salt and pepper to taste

Place grated zucchini in colander. Sprinkle with salt and toss. Let stand for 30 minutes. Press out juice. Melt butter in skillet. Add all ingredients and sauté for approximately 5 minutes.

BREADS

Orange Date Nut Bread

A SWEET TEA LOAF

Yields 1 loaf

1   large orange
1   cup chopped dates
1   teaspoon baking soda
1   cup sugar
2   tablespoons butter
1   teaspoon vanilla
1   egg, beaten
2   cups flour
1   teaspoon baking powder
½   teaspoon salt
½   cup chopped walnuts

Grate orange rind. Squeeze juice from orange and combine with enough boiling water to equal 1 cup. Pour into bowl and add rind and dates. Stir in baking soda, sugar, butter, vanilla and egg. Sift together flour, baking powder and salt. Add to mixture, beating thoroughly. Stir in walnuts.

❧   Spoon mixture into greased loaf pan. Bake at 350 degrees for 50 minutes.

❧   Cool completely before removing from pan.

Pumpkin Bread

A DENSE, SPICY BREAD

Yields 2 loaves

3⅓   cups flour
2⅔   cups sugar
½   teaspoon baking powder
2   teaspoons baking soda
1   teaspoon salt
1   teaspoon cinnamon
1   teaspoon cloves
1   teaspoon ginger
2   cups cooked, mashed pumpkin
⅔   cup water
4   eggs, beaten
⅔   cup raisins
⅔   cup chopped nuts

Combine flour, sugar, baking powder, baking soda, salt, cinnamon, cloves and ginger. Blend in pumpkin, water and eggs. Stir in raisins and nuts.

❧   Pour into 2 greased and floured loaf pans. Bake at 350 degrees for 50 to 55 minutes.

Apple Spice Bread

PERFECT FOR BRUNCH OR TEA

Yields 1 loaf

1⅓ cups flour
¾ teaspoon baking soda
½ teaspoon salt
1 teaspoon cinnamon
¼ teaspoon ground cloves
1 cup plus 1 teaspoon sugar
½ cup vegetable oil
2 eggs, beaten
1 teaspoon vanilla extract
2 cups peeled, coarsely chopped apples
½ cup chopped walnuts

Mix together flour, baking soda, salt, cinnamon and cloves. Set aside.

❧ Mix 1 cup sugar with oil in large bowl. Stir in eggs and vanilla, then apples and nuts. Stir in flour mixture. Pour into greased loaf pan.

❧ Bake at 325 degrees for 50 to 60 minutes. After bread has baked for 20 minutes, remove from oven and sprinkle top of bread with 1 teaspoon sugar. Return to oven and finish baking.

Poppy Seed Loaf

A LOVELY CITRUS-GLAZED QUICK BREAD

Yields 2 loaves

3 cups flour
1 teaspoon salt
1½ teaspoons baking powder
1½ cups vegetable oil
2¼ cups sugar
2 tablespoons poppy seeds
3 eggs
1½ cups milk
1 teaspoon almond extract
1½ teaspoons vanilla extract
1 tablespoon butter, melted

Glaze:

1 tablespoon butter, melted
½ teaspoon almond extract
½ teaspoon vanilla extract
¼ cup orange juice
¾ cup sugar

Grease and flour 2 medium loaf pans. Combine all bread ingredients and pour into prepared pans. Bake at 350 degrees for 1 hour.

❧ Combine glaze ingredients in small bowl. Prick hot bread with toothpick. Pour on glaze. Let stand 15 to 20 minutes before removing from pans. Cool completely before slicing.

Lemon Nut Bread

LEMON GIVES THIS SWEET BREAD A TANGY FLAVOR

Yields 1 loaf

1½ cups flour
½ teaspoon salt
1 teaspoon baking powder
½ cup butter, softened
1 cup sugar
2 eggs, slightly beaten
½ cup milk
½ cup chopped pecans
  Grated rind of 1 lemon

Glaze:

¼ cup sugar
  Juice of 1 lemon

Sift flour, salt and baking powder. Set aside.

❧ Cream butter and sugar. Beat in eggs. Add dry ingredients alternately with milk to butter mixture. Beat until smooth. Stir in pecans and lemon rind.

❧ Pour into greased loaf pan. Bake at 350 degrees for 50 minutes or until done.

❧ To glaze bread, combine sugar and lemon juice. Prick hot loaf with toothpick. Pour on glaze. Let stand 15 to 20 minutes. Remove from pan and cool completely before slicing.

Dill Bread

A VERSATILE, AROMATIC BREAD

Yields 2 loaves

2	packages dry yeast
1/2	cup warm water
2	cups cottage cheese
1/4	cup sugar
2	teaspoons salt
2	tablespoons dill seed
2	eggs
2	tablespoons butter, softened
1/2	teaspoon baking soda
2	tablespoons onion flakes
5–6	cups flour

Dissolve yeast in warm water and set aside. In a large bowl, mix together cottage cheese, sugar, salt, dill seed, eggs, butter, baking soda and onion. Add yeast mixture and enough flour to make a soft but not sticky dough.

❧ Place dough on a floured surface and knead for about 10 minutes. Place in a greased bowl, turning to coat on all sides. Cover with a damp towel and let rise in a warm place until dough has doubled, about 1 hour.

❧ Divide dough in half and shape into 2 loaves. Place in greased loaf pans, turning to coat on all sides. Let rise in a warm place until dough doubles in size, about 30 to 45 minutes. Bake at 350 degrees for 40 to 50 minutes.

❧ Let cool 5 minutes. Remove from pans and sprinkle tops with salt.

Oatmeal Bread

ESPECIALLY GOOD TOASTED

Yields 2 loaves

2	cups milk, scalded
2	cups quick oats
1/2	cup brown sugar
2	tablespoons butter, softened
1	teaspoon salt
1	package dry yeast
1/4	cup very warm water
4–5	cups flour

Place milk, oats, brown sugar, butter and salt in mixing bowl and stir. Cool to lukewarm.

❧ Dissolve yeast in warm water. Pour into oat mixture. Beat in 1 1/2 cups flour. Let stand until light and bubbly, approximately 15 minutes.

❧ Gradually add enough of remaining flour so that dough is soft and does not stick to sides of bowl. Knead dough on a lightly floured surface until smooth, about 5 minutes. Place dough in greased bowl and turn to coat on all sides. Cover with damp towel. Let rise in warm place for 1 to 1 1/2 hours.

❧ Punch down dough. Divide in half and shape into loaves. Place in greased loaf pans, turning to coat all sides. Cover with damp towel and let rise until dough doubles in size, about 30 to 40 minutes.

❧ Bake at 400 degrees for 10 minutes. Reduce heat to 375 degrees and bake an additional 30 to 40 minutes.

Pumpernickel Rye Bread

A DARK, ROBUST BREAD

Yields 2 loaves

2	packages dry yeast
1 1/2	cups warm water
2 3/4	cups rye flour
2	teaspoons salt
1	tablespoon caraway seeds
2	tablespoons butter, softened
1/3	cup molasses
4	cups flour
	Cornmeal

Dissolve yeast in warm water. Add rye flour and beat until smooth. Cover and let stand all day or overnight.

❧ Stir in salt, caraway seeds, butter, molasses and 2 cups of flour. Add enough of the remaining flour to make a soft, but not sticky, dough. Place on a lightly floured surface and knead 5 minutes. Place dough in a greased bowl, turning to coat all sides. Cover and let rise in a warm place about 1 hour.

❧ Punch down dough. Divide in half and shape into 2 balls. Place on a cookie sheet which has been sprinkled with cornmeal. Let rise in a warm place until dough has doubled, about 30 to 40 minutes. Brush loaves with cold water.

❧ Bake at 375 degrees for 40 to 45 minutes.

Beer Bread

GREAT WITH STEW OR CHILI

Yields 1 loaf

  3 **cups self-rising flour**
⅓ **cup sugar**
  1 **12-ounce can beer, at room temperature**
2–3 **tablespoons butter, melted**

Mix together flour, sugar and beer to form a thick batter. Spoon into a greased loaf pan. Cover and let rise at room temperature for 1 hour.

❦ Brush top with half the melted butter. Bake at 350 degrees for 1 hour.

❦ Brush top with remaining melted butter. Serve warm.

Pumpkin Chocolate Chip Muffins

CHOCOLATE CHIPS MAKE THESE IRRESISTIBLE

Yields 1 dozen muffins

1⅔ **cups flour**
  1 **cup sugar**
  1 **teaspoon pumpkin pie spice**
  1 **teaspoon cinnamon**
  1 **teaspoon baking soda**
¼ **teaspoon baking powder**
¼ **teaspoon salt**
  2 **large eggs**
  1 **cup canned pumpkin**
½ **cup butter, melted**
  1 **cup chocolate chips**

Thoroughly mix flour, sugar, pie spice, cinnamon, baking soda, baking powder and salt in a large bowl. Beat together eggs, pumpkin and butter. Pour over dry ingredients and mix until just moistened. Add chocolate chips. Spoon batter evenly into greased muffin tins. Bake at 350 degrees for 20 to 25 minutes.

Danish Puff

A SWEET, BUTTERY BREAKFAST PASTRY

Yields 2 loaves

1 **cup butter**
2 **cups sifted flour**
½ **teaspoon almond extract**
3 **eggs**

Frosting:
  Powdered sugar
  Milk

Cut ½ cup butter into 1 cup flour. Add 2 tablespoons water and mix thoroughly. Spread mixture into 2 rectangles measuring 12″ × 3″ on an ungreased cookie sheet.

❦ In large saucepan, bring 1 cup water and remaining ½ cup butter just to a boil. Add almond extract. Remove from heat and beat in remaining 1 cup flour. Add eggs, one at a time, beating well after each addition. Spread over dough mixture.

❦ Bake at 350 degrees until lightly browned, approximately 60 minutes. Frost with a thin icing made from powdered sugar and milk.

Crunchy Corn Biscuits

A GREAT ALTERNATIVE TO CORN BREAD

Yields approximately 24 biscuits

1   8½-ounce can creamed yellow corn
2   cups Bisquick
½   cup butter

Stir corn and Bisquick together. Roll out on lightly floured surface to ¼" thickness. Cut into 2" rounds.

❧   Melt butter in jelly roll pan. Coat both sides of rounds with melted butter and place in same pan. Bake at 450 degrees until golden, about 10 minutes.

Cinnamon Puffs

SERVE THESE INSTEAD OF DOUGHNUTS

Yields 12 puffs

½   cup sugar
⅓   cup butter
1   egg
1½   cups flour
1½   teaspoons baking powder
½   teaspoon salt
½   teaspoon nutmeg
½   cup milk

Topping:
½   cup sugar
1   tablespoon cinnamon
6   tablespoons butter, melted

Cream sugar and butter. Add egg. Sift together flour, baking powder, salt and nutmeg. Add dry ingredients alternately with milk to butter mixture. Beat well after each addition. Spoon batter into greased muffin tins. Bake at 350 degrees for 15 to 20 minutes. Cool 5 minutes, then remove from tins.

❧   For topping, combine sugar and cinnamon in shallow bowl. Dip hot puffs in melted butter, then roll in cinnamon mixture.

Raspberry Muffins

A DIFFERENT AND DELICIOUS
BERRY MUFFIN

Yields 12 muffins or 1 loaf

1½   cups flour
1   cup sugar
½   teaspoon baking soda
½   teaspoon salt
2   teaspoons cinnamon
1   12-ounce package frozen raspberries, thawed and undrained
2   eggs, beaten
⅔   cup vegetable oil
½   cup chopped pecans

Combine flour, sugar, baking soda, salt and cinnamon. Make a well in center of dry ingredients and stir in undrained raspberries, eggs and oil. Mix well. Stir in pecans.

❧   Spoon batter into greased muffin tins. Bake at 400 degrees for 15 to 20 minutes. Cool 5 minutes, then remove from tins.

❧   Recipe can also be baked in a greased and floured loaf pan at 350 degrees for 1 hour or until done.

Syrian Bread

Yields 10 large or 20 small rounds

1   **package dry yeast**
2   **cups warm water**
4   **cups flour**
2   **cups wheat flour**
4   **teaspoons salt**

Dissolve yeast in warm water. Add remaining ingredients. Knead well, about 5 minutes. Place in a lightly greased bowl, turning to coat. Cover with damp towel and let rise in a warm place until dough has doubled, about 1 hour.

❧ Divide dough into 10 large or 20 small balls. Let rise again, 20 to 30 minutes. Roll out each ball into a circle. Bake at 450 degrees directly on oven racks for 4 minutes. Bread will deflate as it cools.

Sweet Cream Biscuits

CREAM MAKES THESE EXTRA RICH

Yields 12 biscuits

2   **cups flour**
1   **teaspoon salt**
1   **tablespoon baking powder**
2   **teaspoons sugar**
1   **cup heavy cream**
¼   **cup butter, melted**

Sift together dry ingredients. Stir in cream until mixture becomes a soft dough that can be handled easily.

❧ Knead dough for 1 minute on a floured surface, then pat to ½″ to ¾″ thickness.

❧ Cut dough in rounds or squares. Dip in melted butter and place on greased baking sheet.

❧ Bake at 425 degrees for 15 to 18 minutes.

Old-Fashioned Popovers

A TRADITIONAL ACCOMPANIMENT TO
ROASTS OR SOUPS

Yields 8–10 popovers

6   **eggs, slightly beaten**
2   **cups milk**
6   **tablespoons butter, melted**
2   **cups sifted flour**
1   **teaspoon salt**

Blend together eggs, milk and butter. Gradually stir in flour and salt. Pour into greased popover pans or custard cups to within ¼″ of top. Place on cookie sheet for baking.

❧ Bake at 375 degrees for 50 minutes. Slit sides with sharp knife and return to oven for 10 minutes until tops are firm and brown. Remove immediately from pans, using knife to loosen if necessary.

Wooden Shoes

THIS UNUSUAL BREAKFAST PUFF RISES TO
RESEMBLE TWO WOODEN SHOES

Serves 4

2   tablespoons butter
1   cup flour
¾   cup milk
½   teaspoon salt
3   eggs

Melt butter in a 9″ square baking pan. Mix flour, milk, salt and eggs. Pour mixture into pan. Bake at 425 degrees for 20 minutes.

❧ Serve with butter and powdered sugar or jam.

TEA

ASSORTED TEA SANDWICHES
RASPBERRY MUFFINS ❧ PUMPKIN BREAD
SWEET CREAM BISCUITS
LEMON NUT BREAD

Stromboli Bread

A BAKED SANDWICH IDEAL FOR A CROWD

Serves 6–8

1 **package frozen bread dough (2 loaves)**
1 **large clove garlic, minced**
3 **tablespoons olive oil**
¼ **pound pepperoni, thinly sliced**
¼ **pound salami, thinly sliced**
¼ **pound mozzarella cheese, shredded**
¼ **pound Parmesan cheese, shredded**
¼ **pound provolone cheese, shredded**
 Italian peppers, hot or mild, as desired

Defrost bread dough. Roll each loaf into a large rectangle on a lightly floured surface. Mix together garlic and oil and brush on bread.

❧ Alternate layers of meat, cheeses and peppers on tops of loaves. Roll lengthwise jellyroll style. Bread may be wrapped and frozen at this time until ready to be defrosted and baked.

❧ Bake at 350 degrees for 20 minutes, or until brown on top. Slice with very sharp bread knife.

Calzone d'Umberto

A FABULOUS ALTERNATIVE TO PIZZA

Serves 6

Dough:
1 **package active dry yeast**
1½ **cups warm water**
4 **cups flour**
1 **teaspoon salt**
¼ **cup olive oil**

Filling:
1 **package frozen artichoke hearts, cooked and drained**
¼ **pound pepperoni, sliced**
¼ **pound ham, chopped**
¼ **pound mushrooms, sliced**
1 **small onion, chopped**
1 **tomato, seeded and chopped**
6 **ounces mozzarella cheese, grated**
4 **ounces Parmesan cheese, grated**
6 **tablespoons tomato sauce**

Dissolve yeast in ¼ cup warm water. Let stand for 10 minutes.

❧ Combine flour and salt in large bowl. Make a well in center of flour mixture and pour in yeast mixture; add remaining water and oil. Mix with fork until dough can be formed into a ball.

❧ Transfer to floured board and knead until smooth and elastic, approximately 15 minutes. Place in bowl and cover with plastic wrap or damp cloth. Place bowl in warm place and let rise until dough has doubled, approximately 1½ hours.

❧ Punch down dough and separate into 6 equal parts. Roll each part into a circle on a floured board. Keep unrolled parts covered with damp cloth.

❧ Combine artichoke hearts, pepperoni, ham, mushrooms, onion, tomato, mozzarella, Parmesan and tomato sauce.

❧ Place some of filling mixture on half of dough. Lightly rub water along edge of dough. Fold over and press edges together. Cut 3 small slits across top of turnover. Repeat process with remaining dough.

❧ Place on ungreased cookie sheet and bake at 500 degrees for 8 to 10 minutes.

Herbed Garlic Bread

1   large loaf Italian or French bread, split lengthwise

¾   cup butter, softened

4   scallions, including tops, finely chopped

1   clove garlic, crushed

½   teaspoon marjoram

½   teaspoon oregano

1   3-ounce can chopped ripe olives, drained well

½   cup grated Parmesan cheese

Paprika

Combine butter, scallions, garlic, marjoram, oregano and olives. Spread mixture evenly over bread. Sprinkle with Parmesan cheese and paprika.

❧ Bake at 350 degrees until heated through. Broil 1 to 2 minutes to toast. Slice into serving pieces. May also be served as an appetizer if cut into smaller pieces.

Goat Cheese Pizza

3   tablespoons very warm water

3   tablespoons milk

½   package active dry yeast

Pinch of sugar

2   tablespoons olive oil, plus additional for brushing dough

¼   teaspoon salt

¾   cup unbleached white flour (use up to 1¼ cups to make soft dough)

2   cloves garlic, finely minced

Topping:

2   tablespoons extra virgin olive oil

1   small red onion, thinly sliced

2   cloves garlic, finely minced

Salt and pepper to taste

2–3   ounces mozzarella cheese, grated

3½   ounces goat cheese, softened

12   Niçoise or small green olives, pitted and quartered

2   sun-dried tomatoes in oil, julienned

Chopped parsley, thyme and basil

Combine water and milk. Add yeast and sugar and stir until yeast dissolves. Mix in olive oil and salt, then gradually add flour, stirring to make a soft dough. Add just enough flour to keep dough from sticking to surface. Knead for 5 minutes on a lightly floured surface. Place dough in oiled bowl and turn so entire surface is coated. Cover bowl and let dough rise in a warm place until it has doubled, approximately 30 to 45 minutes.

❧ When dough has doubled in bulk, form into a ball and roll out on a floured surface. Pick up dough, stretching and shaping it to form a 10″ round, approximately ⅛″ thick, rolling out as necessary. The edges should be slightly thicker to contain the topping. Brush with a mixture of oil and garlic.

❧ To prepare topping, heat olive oil in skillet and sauté onion for a few minutes until soft and translucent. Add garlic and season with salt and pepper. Cook another 2 to 3 minutes.

❧ When dough is shaped and oiled, cover with the sautéed onions and the mozzarella cheese. Sprinkle lumps of goat cheese, olives and tomatoes over dough. Slide pizza onto a preheated stone or cookie sheet and bake at 500 degrees for 8 to 12 minutes or until the edges are well browned. Remove from oven and garnish top with fresh parsley, thyme and basil.

DESSERTS

Poppy Seed Cake

A SUBTLY SWEET BREAKFAST OR TEA CAKE

Serves 12

1½ cups sugar
1 cup butter
2 eggs
1 teaspoon baking powder
4 tablespoons poppy seeds
1 cup sour cream
1 teaspoon vanilla
2 cups sifted flour
½ teaspoon baking soda

Cream sugar, butter and eggs. Add remaining ingredients. Beat mixture for 5 minutes. Pour into greased tube pan.

❦ Bake at 350 degrees for 1 hour. If desired, glaze or dust with powdered sugar.

Whipped Cream Pound Cake

LIGHT WITH A DELICATE CRUST

Serves 10–12

1 cup butter
3 cups sugar
3 cups flour
6 eggs
1 cup heavy cream
2 teaspoons vanilla or 2 tablespoons orange liqueur

Cream butter and sugar. Alternately add flour and eggs, 2 at a time. Whip cream until soft peaks form. Add vanilla or orange liqueur and fold into batter. Pour into greased and floured bundt pan and bake at 325 degrees for 1 hour and 20 minutes or until done.

Potomac Pound Cake

GREAT WITH FRESH FRUIT OR ICE CREAM

Serves 12

1   cup butter, softened
3   cups sugar
6   large eggs
½   teaspoon vanilla
¼   teaspoon orange extract
¼   teaspoon lemon extract
3   cups flour
½   teaspoon baking soda
¼   teaspoon salt
1   cup sour cream

Cream butter and sugar. Beat in eggs 1 at a time. Add vanilla and orange and lemon extracts.

❧ In separate bowl, sift together flour, baking soda and salt. Alternately add flour mixture and sour cream to butter mixture. Beat at medium speed for 10 minutes.

❧ Pour into greased 10″ tube pan or 2 loaf pans. Bake at 350 degrees for 1¼ hours for tube pan or 1 hour for loaf pans.

Heavenly Devil's Food Cake

AN EXTRA RICH
THREE-LAYER CAKE

Serves 10–12

1   cup unsweetened cocoa
2   cups boiling water
2¾ cups sifted flour
2   teaspoons baking soda
½   teaspoon salt
½   teaspoon baking powder
1   cup butter, softened
2½ cups sugar
4   eggs
1½ teaspoons vanilla

Filling:
1   cup heavy cream, chilled
¼   cup powdered sugar
1   teaspoon vanilla

Frosting:
1   6-ounce package semisweet chocolate chips
½   cup light cream
1   cup butter
2½ cups powdered sugar

Combine cocoa and boiling water and beat until smooth. Cool completely.

❧ Sift together flour, soda, salt and baking powder. Set aside.

❧ In large bowl, cream butter, sugar, eggs and vanilla until light, about 5 minutes. Add flour mixture alternately with cocoa mixture, beginning and ending with flour mixture. Do not overbeat.

❧ Grease and lightly flour 3 9″ cake pans. Divide cake batter evenly between pans. Bake at 350 degrees for 25 to 30 minutes or until cake springs back when gently touched. Cool in pans for 10 minutes. Carefully loosen sides with knife and remove. Cool completely.

❧ To make filling, whip cream until soft peaks form. Beat in sugar and vanilla. Refrigerate.

❧ To make frosting, combine chocolate chips, cream and butter in saucepan. Stir over medium heat until smooth. Remove from heat and whisk in powdered sugar. Place pan over ice and beat until frosting holds its shape.

❧ To assemble cake, place 1 layer topside down on a plate. Spread with half the cream filling. Repeat with second layer. Place third layer on top with topside up.

❧ Frost cake and refrigerate at least 1 hour before serving.

Fruity Bundt Cake

FRUITS AND NUTS ADD A WONDERFUL
TEXTURE

Serves 10–12

- 3 **cups flour**
- 2 **teaspoons cinnamon**
- 1 **teaspoon baking soda**
- ½ **teaspoon salt**
- 2 **cups sugar**
- 1½ **cups vegetable oil**
- 1 **8-ounce can crushed pineapple, undrained**
- 1 **cup shredded coconut**
- 2 **bananas, mashed**
- 1 **cup chopped pecans**
- 1½ **teaspoons vanilla**
- 3 **eggs**

Sift together flour, cinnamon, baking soda, salt and sugar. Mix by hand remaining ingredients, blending thoroughly. Stir in flour mixture and pour into greased and floured bundt pan.

❧ Bake at 325 degrees for approximately 1 hour and 20 minutes.

Old-Fashioned Strawberry Shortcake

A SUMMER TRADITION

Serves 6–8

- 2 **cups flour**
- 5 **tablespoons sugar**
- 4 **teaspoons baking powder**
- 1 **teaspoon salt**
- ⅓ **cup butter, softened**
- ⅔ **cup milk**
- 2 **pints fresh ripe strawberries**
- 1 **cup heavy cream**

Combine flour, 2 tablespoons sugar, baking powder and salt. With fork or pastry blender, cut butter into flour mixture until it resembles coarse meal. Using fork, stir in milk until just blended. Place dough on lightly floured surface and knead 10 times. Dough will be crumbly. Pat dough evenly into greased and lightly floured 8″ round cake pan. Bake at 425 degrees until lightly golden, approximately 13 to 15 minutes. Cool shortcake for 5 minutes, then remove from pan and cool completely on wire rack.

❧ Hull and slice strawberries, reserving several whole berries for garnish. Toss sliced berries with 2 tablespoons sugar and set aside. Cut cooled shortcake in half horizontally. Beat cream and remaining 1 tablespoon sugar until soft peaks form.

❧ Place bottom layer of shortcake on serving platter, cut side up. Drizzle juice from berries over surface. Spread with half the whipped cream. Arrange berries over cream. Place top shortcake layer over berries and spoon remaining whipped cream decoratively over center of cake. Garnish with reserved whole strawberries.

Carrot Cake

DATES AND COCONUT ADD A NEW TWIST

Serves 12

- 2 **cups sifted flour**
- 2 **teaspoons baking soda**
- 3 **cups grated carrots**
- ¾ **cup shredded coconut**
- 1 **teaspoon salt**
- 1 **cup chopped dates**
- ½ **cup chopped nuts**
- 2 **teaspoons cinnamon**
- 2 **cups sugar**
- 1½ **cups vegetable oil**
- 1 **teaspoon vanilla**
- 4 **eggs, slightly beaten**

Frosting:

- 8 **ounces cream cheese, softened**
- ¼ **cup butter**
- 1 **teaspoon vanilla**
- 1¾ **cups powdered sugar**

Combine flour, baking soda, carrots, coconut, salt, dates, nuts, cinnamon and sugar. Stir in vegetable oil, vanilla and eggs. Pour into greased and floured 10″ × 14″ baking pan. Bake at 350 degrees for approximately 1 hour. Allow cake to cool before frosting.

❧ To make frosting, cream together cream cheese and butter until fluffy. Blend in vanilla and powdered sugar.

Hazelnut Meringues with Raspberry Sauce

LIGHT AND SPECIAL

Serves 5–6

- 1 **tablespoon butter, melted**
- 1 **tablespoon flour**
- 5 **ounces hazelnuts**
- 4 **egg whites**
- 1 **cup sugar**
- ¼ **teaspoon vanilla**
- ½ **teaspoon white vinegar**
  Powdered sugar
- 1 **cup heavy cream**

Raspberry Sauce:

- 1 **10-ounce package frozen raspberries**
  Lemon juice to taste
  Powdered sugar to taste

Brush cookie sheet with melted butter and dust with flour.

❧ Set aside 5 hazelnuts. Grind remaining nuts, being careful not to overgrind as they will become too greasy and make the meringue heavy. Weigh out exactly 3½ ounces ground hazelnuts for the meringue.

❧ Beat egg whites until stiff peaks form. Gradually beat in sugar, vanilla and white vinegar until very stiff. With a large spoon, gently fold in ground hazelnuts.

❧ Divide mixture in half and spread each mound to about 1½″ thickness on cookie sheet.

❧ Bake at 375 degrees for 35 minutes. Allow to cool several minutes, then transfer to wire rack and cool completely.

❧ For sauce, purée raspberries in food processor or blender, adding a few drops lemon juice and a little powdered sugar until desired sweetness is achieved. Pour through sieve. If sauce is too thick, add water.

❧ Whip cream until soft peaks form. Spread two-thirds of whipped cream onto 1 of the cooled meringues, then place other meringue on top. Dust with powdered sugar. Decorate edge of meringue with 5 rosettes of whipped cream, placing a hazelnut atop each. Serve raspberry sauce on the side.

Chocolate Chiffon Cake

A CHOCOLATE-FLECKED
SPONGE CAKE

Serves 10–12

2 **cups flour**
1¾ **cups sugar**
3 **teaspoons baking powder**
1 **teaspoon salt**
½ **cup vegetable oil**
7 **eggs, separated**
¾ **cup cold water**
2 **teaspoons vanilla**
½ **teaspoon cream of tartar**
3 **ounces semisweet chocolate, coarsely grated**

In large bowl, sift together flour, sugar, baking powder and salt. Make a well in flour mixture and add oil, egg yolks, cold water and vanilla. Beat until smooth.

❧ Beat egg whites until very stiff. Beat in cream of tartar. Gently fold egg whites into cake mixture. Fold grated chocolate into batter.

❧ Pour batter into greased 10″ tube pan. Bake at 325 degrees for 55 minutes, then bake at 350 degrees for 10 to 15 minutes. Immediately turn pan upside down and cool.

Cassata alla Siciliana

FRUITED RICOTTA FILLING MOISTENS
THIS CAKE

Serves 8

1 **9″ × 3″ pound cake**
1 **pound ricotta cheese**
2 **tablespoons heavy cream**
¼ **cup sugar**
3 **tablespoons Grand Marnier**
3 **tablespoons chopped candied fruit**
2 **ounces semisweet chocolate, chopped**

Frosting:

12 **ounces semisweet chocolate, chopped**
¾ **cup strong black coffee**
1 **cup unsalted butter, chilled and cut into ½″ pieces**

Slice crust off top and ends of pound cake. Cut cake horizontally into ½″ slices, creating several layers.

❧ Force ricotta cheese through sieve to remove lumps. Beat cheese with mixer until smooth. Gradually beat in cream, sugar and Grand Marnier. Mix well. Fold in candied fruit and chocolate.

❧ To make frosting, combine chocolate pieces and coffee in double boiler. Stir constantly until chocolate has melted. Remove from heat. Beat in butter, piece by piece, until mixture is smooth. Chill frosting until it is thick enough to spread.

❧ To assemble cake, place bottom slice of pound cake on plate. Spread ricotta cheese mixture on top. Repeat process with additional slices and top with last slice of cake. Chill until ricotta is firm, approximately 2 hours. Frost cake. Cover loosely with foil and refrigerate 1 day before serving.

Lemon Cheesecake

A TART, CUSTARDLIKE CHEESECAKE

Serves 12–14

Crust:

- ¾ cup butter
- 1¼ cups flour
- ¼ cup sugar
- 1 egg yolk
  Rind of ½ lemon, grated

Filling:

- 5 8-ounce packages cream cheese, softened
- 1¾ cups sugar
- 3 tablespoons flour
  Rind of 1½ lemons, grated
- 5 whole eggs
- 2 egg yolks

Blend together crust ingredients. Shape into ball, wrap and chill overnight.

❦ Soften chilled dough and press ⅓ of dough into bottom of 10″ springform pan. Bake at 400 degrees for 8 minutes. Cool.

❦ For filling, beat cream cheese until smooth. Blend in sugar and beat until fluffy. Blend in flour, lemon rind, eggs and egg yolks. Beat for 5 minutes.

❦ Press remaining dough around sides of pan. Pour in cream cheese mixture. Bake at 475 degrees for 12 minutes. Reduce temperature to 300 degrees and bake 40 minutes. Turn oven off, leaving cheesecake in oven for 30 minutes. Chill.

Lemon Almond Torte

THE PERFECT ENDING TO A SPECIAL DINNER

Serves 10–12

- 1 cup unsalted butter
- 1 cup sugar
- 1½ cups finely ground blanched almonds
- 4 large eggs, at room temperature
- 1 teaspoon vanilla
- 1 teaspoon lemon extract
- 1 teaspoon almond extract
- 1 tablespoon grated lemon rind
- 1 cup flour
- 1 teaspoon baking powder
- ¼ teaspoon salt
- ¼ cup lemon juice
  Candied lemon peel or whole almonds for garnish

Glaze:

- ¼ cup lemon juice
- 2 cups powdered sugar

Cream butter, sugar and 1 cup almonds until fluffy. Add eggs 1 at a time. Beat in vanilla, lemon and almond extracts and lemon rind. Sift together dry ingredients and add to batter, alternating with lemon juice.

❦ Pour batter into greased 8″ springform pan. Bake at 350 degrees for 50 minutes. Cool cake for 15 minutes before releasing springform.

❦ Whisk together glaze ingredients. Spread evenly over top and sides of cake. Sprinkle remaining almonds onto sides of glazed cake. Garnish with candied lemon peel or whole almonds.

Best Ever Cheesecake

GARNISH WITH FRESH FRUIT

Serves 10–12

Crust:

20   graham crackers, crushed into crumbs

¼   cup sugar

½   cup butter, melted

Filling:

3   8-ounce packages cream cheese, softened

1½   cups sugar

⅛   teaspoon salt

4   eggs

1   teaspoon vanilla

Topping:

1   pint sour cream

¼   cup sugar

2   teaspoons vanilla

    Raspberries, blueberries or strawberries for garnish, if desired

Combine cracker crumbs with sugar and melted butter. Press into bottom and sides of 9″ springform pan. Chill.

❧ For filling, beat cream cheese until smooth. Blend in sugar and salt and beat until fluffy. Add eggs 1 at a time. Add vanilla. Pour into crust and bake at 350 degrees for 50 to 60 minutes or until center is firm. Remove from oven and let stand for 15 minutes.

❧ For topping, combine sour cream, sugar and vanilla. Spread over cheesecake. Bake at 450 degrees for 10 minutes until top is set. Chill and garnish.

Portuguese Almond Cake

A DENSE CAKE WITH A CRUNCHY
ALMOND TOPPING

Serves 8

1   cup sifted flour

¾   cup sugar

½   teaspoon baking powder

½   teaspoon baking soda

¼   teaspoon salt

1   egg

½   cup buttermilk

½   teaspoon vanilla

⅓   cup butter, melted and cooled to room temperature

⅔   cup sliced almonds

Hot Almond Syrup:

¾   cup sugar

6   tablespoons water

½   teaspoon lemon juice

½   teaspoon almond extract

Sift together flour, sugar, baking powder, baking soda and salt.

❧ In separate bowl, beat egg, buttermilk and vanilla until smooth. Stir in butter. Add to flour mixture and blend until nearly smooth.

❧ Turn mixture into greased 9″ spring-form pan. Bake at 350 degrees about 35 minutes, or until center of cake springs back when touched lightly. Remove cake from oven and, while still hot, sprinkle with almonds.

❧ To make syrup, combine sugar, water and lemon juice in 1-quart saucepan. Boil until mixture reaches 220 degrees Farenheit on candy thermometer. Do not overcook or syrup will harden on cake. Remove from heat and add almond extract. Slowly pour evenly over cake, allowing syrup to soak in. Broil about 6″ from heat until almonds are lightly toasted.

❧ Cool cake 10 minutes. Using knife, loosen edges between pan and cake. Cool completely before releasing springform.

French Double Chocolate Pie

INTENSELY CHOCOLATE

Serves 8–12

Crust:

- ¾ cup unsalted butter, softened
- 1 teaspoon cinnamon
- 3 cups chocolate wafer crumbs

Filling:

- 12 squares semisweet chocolate
- 7 eggs
- 5–7 tablespoons amber rum
- ⅛ teaspoon salt
- 1½ cups heavy cream

Combine butter, cinnamon and wafer crumbs until well blended. Press mixture onto bottom of buttered 10″ pie plate. Bake at 350 degrees for 3 minutes. Cool.

❧ For filling, melt chocolate over low heat, stirring constantly. Cool. Beat 2 whole eggs and 5 egg yolks in large bowl until thick and light. Stir in cooled chocolate, rum and salt.

❧ Beat 5 egg whites until soft peaks form. Fold chocolate mixture into egg whites. Whip 1 cup cream until stiff. Fold into chocolate mixture and spoon into cooled crust. Chill until set, about 3 hours.

❧ Whip remaining half cup cream until stiff and pipe through pastry tube or spoon on pie as garnish. Chocolate curls may be added as additional garnish.

Chocolate Mousse Torte

A HEAVENLY DESSERT

Serves 10–12

Crust:

- 3 cups chocolate wafer crumbs
- ½ cup plus 2 tablespoons butter, melted

Filling:

- 1 pound semisweet chocolate
- 6 eggs
- 2 cups heavy cream
- 6 tablespoons powdered sugar

Topping:

- 2 cups heavy cream
- 3 tablespoons powdered sugar

Combine crust ingredients and press on bottom and sides of a 10″ springform pan. Refrigerate 30 minutes.

❧ Melt chocolate in double boiler. Cool until lukewarm. Add 2 eggs and mix well. Separate remaining 4 eggs. Add yolks to chocolate mixture and blend well.

❧ Whip cream with sugar until soft peaks form. In separate bowl, beat egg whites until soft, but not dry. Stir a small amount of whipped cream and egg whites into the chocolate mixture. Alternately fold in remaining whipped cream and egg whites. Turn into crust and chill at least 6 hours, or overnight.

❧ For topping, beat cream with powdered sugar until stiff. Loosen springform pan and remove pie. Cover top with all but ½ cup of cream. Place reserved cream in a tube and pipe rosettes onto middle and top edge of pie.

Tart Shell

CRISP AND DELICATE ENOUGH FOR
ANY FILLING

Yields 1 tart shell

1¼   **cups plus 2 tablespoons flour**
¼   **cup sugar**
½   **cup unsalted butter, cut into bits and frozen**
1   **egg yolk**
2   **tablespoons heavy cream**

Place flour, sugar and frozen butter in food processor or blender. Process until mixture resembles fine crumbs.

In separate dish, stir together egg yolk and cream. Pour into work bowl with crumb mixture. Process until mixture forms a ball. Refrigerate dough for 30 minutes.

Roll out dough. Cut to fit 8″ to 10″ tart pan. Freeze dough for at least 30 minutes before baking.

Directly from freezer, prick bottom and sides of dough with fork. Cover pastry with waxed paper and weight with beans or pastry weights. Bake on center rack of oven at 400 degrees for 15 minutes. Remove waxed paper and weights and continue baking for 10 to 15 minutes.

Unbaked tart pastry can be frozen for months. Freeze dough in ball or in tart pan, covered tightly.

Fluffy Pumpkin Pie

THE HINT OF RUM ADDS PANACHE
TO A HOLIDAY FAVORITE

Serves 12–16

3½   **cups cooked or canned pumpkin**
1   **cup light brown sugar**
1   **cup plus 2 tablespoons sugar**
1   **teaspoon salt**
3   **tablespoons light molasses**
3   **tablespoons dark rum**
3   **teaspoons cinnamon**
3   **teaspoons ginger**
¼   **teaspoon nutmeg**
¼   **teaspoon cloves**
4   **egg yolks**
1   **cup heavy cream**
¾   **cup milk**
5   **egg whites**
⅛   **teaspoon salt**
2   **9″ unbaked pie shells**

Blend together pumpkin, brown sugar, 1 cup sugar, salt, molasses, rum, cinnamon, ginger, nutmeg, cloves, egg yolks, cream and milk.

In separate bowl, beat egg whites until foamy. Add salt and beat to soft peaks. Gradually add remaining 2 tablespoons sugar and beat until stiff peaks form.

Beat a quarter of the egg whites into pumpkin mixture, then gently fold in remaining egg whites. Ladle pumpkin mixture into pie shells, filling to rim.

Bake at 400 degrees for 15 minutes or until crust is very lightly browned. Reduce heat to 350 degrees and bake for 15 minutes. Lower heat to 325 degrees and continue baking for 15 minutes or until edges are done. Turn off oven, leave door ajar and let pie sit for 20 to 30 minutes.

Serve pie with whipped cream flavored with rum or brandy.

Kentucky Pie

QUICK, EASY AND ABSOLUTELY DELICIOUS

Serves 6–8

½ cup butter, melted and cooled
2 eggs, slightly beaten
1 cup sugar
½ cup flour
1 teaspoon vanilla
1 cup semisweet chocolate chips
1 9″ unbaked pie shell

Mix together butter, eggs, sugar, flour and vanilla until well blended. Stir in chocolate chips and pour into unbaked pie shell.

❧ Bake at 350 degrees for 45 minutes.

Classic Apple Pie

THE ALL-AMERICAN FAVORITE

Serves 6–8

Pastry:
2¼ cups flour, sifted
1½ teaspoons salt
⅓ cup milk
½ cup plus 1 tablespoon vegetable oil

Apple Filling:
7 Granny Smith apples, sliced
1½ cups sugar
⅛ teaspoon salt
¾ teaspoon cinnamon
½ teaspoon nutmeg
2 tablespoons flour
2 tablespoons lemon juice
1 teaspoon grated lemon peel
1 tablespoon butter

Combine flour and salt. Whisk together milk and oil and pour into flour. Stir lightly until mixed.

❧ Separate dough into 2 balls. Roll out each ball between sheets of waxed paper. Place 1 crust in 9″ pie plate. Set aside second crust.

❧ Layer apples in circle over pie shell, working from outside edge towards center. Continue until pie shell is covered and packed with apples.

❧ Combine sugar, salt, cinnamon, nutmeg and flour and sprinkle over apples. Sprinkle with lemon juice and peel. Dot with butter.

❧ Fit second crust on top of pie. Press top and bottom crust edges together, trimming excess dough. Flute edge. Prick top crust all over with fork.

❧ Place pie on cookie sheet. Bake at 500 degrees for 8 minutes. Reduce heat to 350 degrees and bake for 1 hour.

Orchard Apple Pie

SIMPLE AND SWEET WITH A
PECAN CRUMB TOPPING

Serves 6

6–7	tart apples
1	cup sugar
2	tablespoons flour
1	teaspoon cinnamon
1/4	teaspoon nutmeg
1/4	teaspoon salt
1	9″ unbaked pie shell

Crumb Topping:

3/4	cup flour
1/2	cup firmly packed brown sugar
6	tablespoons butter
1/3	cup chopped pecans

Peel apples and slice thin. Combine sugar, flour, cinnamon, nutmeg and salt and mix with apples. Fill pie shell with apple mixture. Bake at 400 degrees for 25 minutes.

❧ For topping, blend flour with brown sugar. Cut in butter until mixture resembles coarse meal. Stir in chopped pecans. Sprinkle topping on pie. Bake an additional 30 to 35 minutes until browned.

Dumbarton Street, Georgetown

PICNIC

Shrimp Vinaigrette

Marinated Chicken Wings

Vegetable Medley Salad ❧ Dill Bread

Potomac Pound Cake with
Sliced Fresh Fruit

Pecan Pie

AN EXCEPTIONAL PECAN PIE

Serves 8

1 1/4	cups sugar
1/2	cup light corn syrup
1/4	cup butter, softened
3	eggs, slightly beaten
1	cup chopped pecans
1	teaspoon vanilla
1	9″ unbaked pie shell

Combine sugar, corn syrup and butter in saucepan. Bring to a boil over high heat, stirring constantly until butter melts completely. Remove from heat and gradually stir hot syrup into beaten eggs. Add pecans. Cool to lukewarm and add vanilla.

❧ Pour mixture into unbaked pie shell. Bake at 350 degrees for 40 to 45 minutes.

Lace Cookies

DELICATE COOKIES WITH AN INTENSE
BUTTERY-ALMOND FLAVOR

Yields 4–5 dozen

1　cup regular or quick oats
1　cup sugar
3　tablespoons flour
¼　teaspoon baking powder
½　teaspoon salt
½　cup butter, melted
1　teaspoon almond extract
1　egg, beaten

Mix together oats, sugar, flour, baking powder and salt. Stir in butter, almond extract and egg.

❧　Refrigerate at least 6 hours, preferably overnight.

❧　Line baking sheet with aluminum foil. Drop batter by teaspoon onto aluminum foil. Bake at 325 degrees until golden brown, approximately 10 to 12 minutes.

❧　Allow to cool completely before peeling cookies from foil.

Bavarian Apple Torte

SOPHISTICATED AND NOT TOO SWEET

Serves 8–10

Crust:
½　cup butter, softened
⅓　cup sugar
½　teaspoon vanilla
1　cup flour

Filling:
8　ounces cream cheese
¼　cup sugar
1　egg, slightly beaten
½　teaspoon vanilla

Topping:
4　cups apples, peeled, cored and sliced
½　teaspoon cinnamon
⅓　cup sugar
½　cup sliced almonds

For crust, cream butter, sugar and vanilla. Slowly stir in flour until mixture forms soft dough. Press dough onto bottom and 1½″ up sides of ungreased 9″ or 10″ springform pan.

❧　For filling, beat cream cheese and sugar. Add egg and vanilla. Blend until smooth. Pour mixture into pan.

❧　For topping, combine apples, cinnamon and sugar. Layer evenly over cream cheese mixture. Sprinkle almonds over top.

❧　Bake at 450 degrees for 10 minutes; lower heat to 400 degrees and bake an additional 25 minutes. Cool completely before removing sides of pan. Serve at room temperature or chilled.

Viennese Crescents

PERFECT FOR GIFT GIVING

Yields 3 dozen

1 cup butter
¼ cup sugar
2 cups flour
1 cup ground almonds
1 teaspoon vanilla
  Powdered sugar

Cream butter thoroughly. Mix in sugar, flour, almonds and vanilla. Shape into crescents and place on greased cookie sheets. Bake at 300 degrees for 30 to 35 minutes.

❦ When cool, roll crescents in powdered sugar.

Brown Butter Shortbread

WONDERFUL WITH CHEESE AND FRUIT

Yields 2 dozen

1 cup butter
½ teaspoon lemon juice
¾ cup sugar
2 tablespoons milk
2 teaspoons vanilla
2 cups flour
1 teaspoon baking powder
½ teaspoon salt

Prepare pan of ice water. Melt butter and continue cooking until it smells like caramel and is almost ready to burn, approximately 10 minutes. When butter suddenly turns amber, plunge pan into ice water. Stir in lemon juice and let sit until solidified, approximately 30 to 45 minutes.

❦ Once butter is solid, beat in sugar until fluffy. Beat in remaining ingredients. Knead on lightly floured surface 10 to 12 times until smooth. Roll into small balls. Place balls on cookie sheet and flatten with fork.

❦ Bake at 300 degrees for 30 minutes.

Scotch Shortbread

EXTRA SPECIAL WHEN CUT INTO
HEART SHAPES

Yields approximately 80 small cookies

1 cup butter
½ cup sugar
2½ cups sifted flour

Combine butter and sugar until well blended. Stir in flour. Chill dough several hours or overnight.

❦ On lightly floured surface, roll out dough to ¼" thickness. Cut into desired shapes with cookie cutter or press into shortbread molds.

❦ Bake at 300 degrees for 20 to 25 minutes or until very lightly browned.

Sugar Crisps

DELICATE COOKIES, IDEAL FOR
DECORATING

Yields 5 dozen

½ cup butter
½ cup margarine
½ cup sugar
½ cup powdered sugar
1 egg
2 teaspoons vanilla
2¼ cups flour
½ teaspoon baking soda
½ teaspoon cream of tartar
⅛ teaspoon salt
   Granulated sugar

Cream together butter, margarine and sugars. Beat in egg and vanilla. Add dry ingredients and beat well.

❦ Shape into 1″ balls and place on greased cookie sheet. Dip bottom of glass in granulated sugar and press balls flat. Bake at 375 degrees for 10 to 12 minutes.

Melting Moments

COOKIES WITH A RICH PECAN TASTE

Yields approximately 5 dozen

1 cup butter, melted and cooled 15 minutes
1 cup brown sugar
1 egg, slightly beaten
1¾ cups flour
½ teaspoon salt
1 teaspoon baking soda
½ teaspoon baking powder
1 teaspoon vanilla
1 cup chopped pecans

Combine butter, brown sugar and egg. Sift together flour, salt, baking soda and baking powder. Add to butter mixture and blend thoroughly. Stir in vanilla and chopped pecans.

❦ Drop dough by teaspoons onto ungreased cookie sheet and flatten with fork.

❦ Bake at 350 degrees for 8 to 10 minutes, or until light brown. Cool completely before removing from cookie sheet.

Molasses Sugar Cookies

A SUGAR AND SPICE COMBINATION

Yields 3 dozen

¾ cup butter, melted
1 cup sugar
⅓ cup molasses
1 egg
2 teaspoons baking soda
½ teaspoon ground cloves
½ teaspoon ground ginger
1 teaspoon cinnamon
½ teaspoon salt
2 cups flour, less 2 tablespoons
   Granulated sugar

Combine butter, sugar and molasses. Stir in egg. Add baking soda, spices, salt and flour. Chill dough until firm.

❦ Form dough into small balls and roll balls in granulated sugar. Place on ungreased cookie sheet. Bake at 375 degrees for 10 minutes. Do not overbake.

New Orleans Pralines

SWEET INDULGENCE

Yields 2–3 dozen

½ cup milk or cream
2 tablespoons light corn syrup
1 box light brown sugar
1 teaspoon salt
1–2 cups pecan halves
2 tablespoons butter
½ teaspoon vanilla

In heavy pot, combine milk, syrup, sugar, salt and pecans. Cook, stirring constantly, over medium heat to soft ball stage (234 degrees Farenheit on candy thermometer).

❧ Remove from heat. Add butter and vanilla and stir until thick. Drop by teaspoons onto waxed paper atop several layers of newspaper.

Pecan Toffee Bars

A GREAT ALTERNATIVE TO BROWNIES

Yields 24

Crust:
1½ cups sifted flour
¾ cup brown sugar
¾ cup butter

Topping:
2 eggs, beaten
1½ cups brown sugar
1½ teaspoons vanilla
3 tablespoons flour
1½ teaspoons baking powder
½ teaspoon salt
1⅓ cups shredded coconut
1½ cups chopped pecans

For crust, combine flour and brown sugar. Cut in butter until mixture is crumbly. Press into greased 13″ × 9″ baking pan. Bake at 350 degrees for 15 minutes.

❧ Beat together eggs, brown sugar and vanilla. Stir in flour, baking powder and salt. Add coconut and pecans. Mix well. Spread over baked crust. Bake at 350 degrees until topping has browned, approximately 30 minutes. Cool in pan and cut into bars.

Mint Brownies

CREME DE MENTHE LENDS AN EXTRA
TASTE SENSATION

Yields approximately 2 dozen

1 cup sugar
½ cup butter
4 eggs
½ teaspoon salt
1 16-ounce can chocolate syrup
1 teaspoon vanilla

Crème de Menthe Filling:
2 cups powdered sugar
2 tablespoons crème de menthe
½ cup butter

Chocolate Topping:
1 cup semisweet chocolate chips
6 tablespoons butter

Mix together sugar, butter, eggs, flour, salt, chocolate syrup and vanilla. Pour into greased and floured 9″ × 13″ baking pan. Bake at 350 degrees for 30 minutes. Let cool.

❧ Blend together crème de menthe filling ingredients. Spread over brownies. Refrigerate until topping hardens, approximately 15 minutes.

❧ Melt together chocolate topping ingredients. Cool and spread over brownies. Refrigerate brownies until served. Cut brownies on diagonal with knife that has been run under hot water to prevent topping from cracking.

Chocolate-Dipped Spritz Cookies

PERFECT WITH SORBET OR FRESH FRUIT

Yields approximately 8 dozen

1½ cups butter
1 cup sugar
3 egg yolks
1 teaspoon vanilla
½ teaspoon salt
3½ cups sifted flour
4 ounces semisweet chocolate, melted and cooled
1 cup finely chopped pistachios or pecans

Combine butter, sugar, egg yolks, vanilla and salt. Beat until light and fluffy. Sift in sifted flour and stir to make soft dough. At this point, dough may be chilled several hours.

❦ Fit pastry bag with star tip and fill with cookie dough. Pipe dough into 3″ lengths on ungreased cookie sheets. Bake at 375 degrees until they just begin to brown, approximately 8 minutes.

❦ When cookies have cooled, dip ends in chocolate, then roll in chopped nuts. Arrange on waxed paper to set.

Chocolate Chip Oatmeal Cookies

OATS VARY THE TRADITION

Yields approximately 9 dozen

2 cups butter, softened
2 cups sugar
2 cups brown sugar
4 eggs
2 teaspoons vanilla
5 cups quick oats
4 cups flour
1 teaspoon salt
2 teaspoons baking powder
2 teaspoons baking soda
2 12-ounce packages semisweet chocolate chips
3 cups chopped nuts

Cream together butter and sugars. Add eggs and vanilla.

❦ Using blender or food processor, grind oats into powder. Add oats, flour, salt, baking powder and baking soda to creamed mixture. Stir in chocolate chips and nuts.

❦ Drop by tablespoons, about 2″ apart, on ungreased cookie sheets. Bake at 375 degrees for 15 minutes.

Brownie Cupcakes

MOIST, RICH CHOCOLATE BITES

Yields 4 dozen tiny cupcakes or 1½ dozen standard cupcakes

4 ounces unsweetened chocolate
1 cup butter
1½ cups chopped pecans
1 cup flour
1¾ cups sugar
4 eggs, slightly beaten
1 teaspoon vanilla

Melt chocolate and butter over low heat. Stir in pecans and set aside.

❦ Combine flour, sugar, eggs and vanilla. Stir in chocolate mixture. Spoon 1 tablespoon batter into greased tiny muffin tins or 3 tablespoons batter into greased standard muffin tins.

❦ Bake at 325 degrees for 10 to 15 minutes for tiny muffins or 30 to 35 minutes for standard muffins. Cool in pan for 10 minutes before removing.

Chocolate Coconut Cookies

TASTES LIKE A CANDY BAR

Yields 3 dozen squares

2 cups graham cracker crumbs
¼ cup powdered sugar
½ cup plus 2 tablespoons butter, melted
2 cups shredded coconut
1 14-ounce can sweetened condensed milk
1 cup chopped almonds, lightly toasted

Glaze:

¼ cup butter
1 6-ounce package chocolate chips

Mix graham cracker crumbs, sugar and butter. Press into bottom of 9″ × 12″ baking pan. Bake at 325 degrees for 10 minutes.

❧ Mix coconut, milk and almonds. Spread over crumb mixture. Bake at 325 degrees for 10 minutes.

❧ For glaze, melt butter and chocolate chips in double boiler. Spoon over coconut layer. Chill.

White Chocolate Cocomacs

JUMBO COOKIES FOR
WHITE-CHOCOLATE LOVERS

Yields 2 dozen 4″ cookies

¾ cup macadamia nuts
12 ounces white chocolate
2 cups flour
1 teaspoon baking soda
1 teaspoon salt
1 cup unsalted butter, softened
1 cup firmly packed dark brown sugar
¼ cup firmly packed light brown sugar
¼ cup sugar
2 eggs
2½ teaspoons vanilla
1⅓ cups shredded coconut

Rub macadamia nuts between 2 paper towels to remove as much salt as possible. Coarsely chop nuts and white chocolate. Set aside.

❧ Mix together flour, baking soda and salt. In separate bowl, beat together butter and sugars until well blended. Beat in eggs and vanilla until mixture is light and fluffy. Add flour mixture. Stir in coconut, white chocolate and macadamia nuts. Cover and refrigerate at least 2 hours or up to 2 days.

❧ Line baking sheet with parchment. Spoon dough onto baking sheet, allowing approximately ¼ cup dough per cookie. Bake at 350 degrees for 18 to 20 minutes. Cool on wire rack.

Zebra Brownies

CHOCOLATE BROWNIES WITH A
CREAM CHEESE LAYER

Yields 16

8 ounces cream cheese, softened
1⅓ cups sugar
3 eggs
2 ounces unsweetened chocolate
½ cup butter
¼ teaspoon almond extract
¾ cup flour
½ teaspoon salt
½ teaspoon baking powder

Combine cream cheese, ⅓ cup sugar and 1 egg. Set aside.

❧ Melt chocolate and butter over low heat. Beat remaining 2 eggs, 1 cup sugar and almond extract until fluffy. Stir in chocolate mixture. Sift together dry ingredients and add to chocolate mixture.

❧ Pour half chocolate mixture into greased 8″ square baking pan. Spoon cream cheese mixture over chocolate layer and top with remaining chocolate mixture. Bake at 350 degrees for 40 to 50 minutes.

Chocolate Peanut Butter Squares

ESPECIALLY POPULAR WITH CHILDREN

Yields 2–3 dozen

½   **cup plus 1 tablespoon butter**
2   **cups peanut butter**
2¾   **cups powdered sugar**
1   **teaspoon vanilla**
12   **ounces semisweet chocolate chips**

Melt ½ cup butter. Stir in peanut butter, powdered sugar and vanilla. Spread into greased 9″ × 13″ pan.

❧ Melt chocolate chips and remaining 1 tablespoon butter in double boiler, stirring constantly until smooth. Pour chocolate over peanut butter mixture, spreading evenly. Chill and cut into squares.

Cappuccino Dips

A SOPHISTICATED COOKIE

Yields 4 dozen

½   **cup butter, softened**
½   **cup margarine, softened**
⅓   **cup sugar**
½   **cup firmly packed brown sugar**
1   **tablespoon instant coffee**
1   **teaspoon hot water**
2   **ounces unsweetened chocolate, melted**
1   **egg**
2   **cups flour**
1   **teaspoon cinnamon**

Glaze:

1   **cup semisweet chocolate chips**
4   **tablespoons butter**

Cream butter, margarine and sugars. Dissolve instant coffee in hot water and add to mixture. Stir in unsweetened chocolate and egg. Beat well. Stir in flour and cinnamon. Cover and chill at least 1 hour.

❧ Divide dough in half and shape into 2 logs approximately 1½″ in diameter. This is easiest when rolled in waxed paper. Chill several hours or overnight. At this point, logs may be wrapped and frozen up to 2 weeks.

❧ When ready to bake, slice logs into ¼″ slices and place on ungreased cookie sheets. Bake at 325 degrees for 8 to 10 minutes, or until just before edges brown.

❧ While cookies cool, melt semisweet chocolate and butter over warm water. Blend until smooth. Dip half of each cookie in chocolate. Place on waxed paper for chocolate to set.

Chocolate Rum Mousse

SERVE IN FANCY DESSERT CUPS

Serves 6

6 ounces semisweet chocolate chips
⅓ cup strong coffee
2 tablespoons rum
2 eggs, at room temperature
1 cup heavy cream
Grated chocolate for garnish

Melt chocolate chips with coffee in top of double boiler. Remove from heat and stir in rum. Pour chocolate mixture into blender or food processor and add eggs. Blend well.

❧ In separate bowl, whip cream until it forms soft peaks. Remove approximately 2 tablespoons of whipped cream and keep chilled.

❧ Fold chocolate mixture into whipped cream. Spoon into dessert cups and chill for at least 4 hours. When ready to serve, top with reserved whipped cream and garnish with grated chocolate.

Slices of Sin

A FANTASTICALLY RICH DESSERT THAT IMPROVES WITH AGE

Serves 10–12

8 ounces semisweet chocolate
½ cup strong coffee
1 cup butter
1 cup sugar
4 eggs, beaten
1 cup heavy cream
2–3 teaspoons brandy

Line glass loaf pan with buttered foil. In double boiler, melt chocolate in coffee. Add butter and sugar, stirring until butter is melted. Cool mixture. Beat in eggs 1 at a time. Pour mixture into prepared loaf pan. Bake at 350 degrees until crust forms on top, approximately 35 to 45 minutes.

❧ Set loaf pan in enough cool water to come halfway up side of pan. Dessert will rise and fall as it cools. When cool, wrap pan well and refrigerate for at least 2 days or up to 2 weeks.

❧ When ready to serve, beat cream until stiff. Stir in brandy. Unmold loaf and slice into individual servings. Garnish with cream.

Chocolate Delight

MOUSSE LACED WITH WALNUT CRUNCH

Serves 6

6 ounces semisweet chocolate chips
¾ cup scalded milk
2 eggs
3 tablespoons strong hot coffee
2 tablespoons dark rum
½ cup chopped walnuts

In blender, combine chocolate chips, milk, eggs, coffee and rum. Blend at high speed 1½ minutes. Add walnuts and blend 30 seconds longer. Pour mixture into ramekins or stemmed glasses and refrigerate overnight.

❧ Serve topped with whipped cream or coffee ice cream.

Chocolate Soufflé

A GRAND FINALE

Serves 6

4　ounces semisweet chocolate
1　ounce unsweetened chocolate
1　cup milk
6　eggs, separated
½　cup sugar
1　teaspoon very strong coffee
　　Powdered sugar for garnish

Butter a 1½ quart soufflé dish and coat with granulated sugar. Chill.

❧ Cut chocolate into small pieces and melt slowly over low heat. Add milk and stir just to boiling point. Add egg yolks and sugar and stir well. Cook over low heat until thickened. Add coffee and let cool just to lukewarm.

❧ Beat egg whites until stiff. Fold into lukewarm chocolate mixture.

❧ Turn into soufflé dish and bake at 350 degrees for 20 minutes. Sprinkle with powdered sugar and serve immediately.

Ganache Gâteaux with Anglaise Sauce

FROM DESIGN CUISINE CATERERS

Serves 8–10

18　ounces bittersweet chocolate
1½　cups powdered sugar
1½　cups unsalted butter, at room temperature
10　extra large eggs, separated
¼　teaspoon salt
　　Fresh raspberries
　　Anglaise Sauce

Melt chocolate in saucepan over low heat. Add ½ cup sugar and mix well. Add butter, one tablespoon at a time, stirring until melted. Add egg yolks and mix well. Remove from heat.

❧ Beat egg whites and salt until stiff. Add remaining 1 cup sugar and beat until egg whites are glossy. Stir one-third of egg white mixture into chocolate, blending thoroughly. Fold in remaining egg whites.

❧ Line an 8-cup savarin mold with plastic wrap and fill with chocolate mixture. Refrigerate overnight. Remove from refrigerator 30 minutes before serving and unmold onto platter. Fill center with fresh raspberries and serve with Anglaise Sauce.

Anglaise Sauce:
1½　cups half-and-half
1　vanilla bean, split
5　egg yolks
3　tablespoons sugar

Bring half-and-half and vanilla bean to a boil. Be careful not to scorch. Remove vanilla bean.

❧ Whisk egg yolks and sugar together until light and lemon colored. Pour half-and-half mixture over yolk mixture, whisking constantly.

❧ Return mixture to heat and cook until slightly thickened, stirring constantly. Pour sauce through strainer into chilled bowl. Refrigerate.

Toffee Squares

SHORTBREAD GLAZED WITH
MILK CHOCOLATE

Yields 4 dozen

1 cup butter
1 cup brown sugar
1 egg yolk
1 teaspoon vanilla
2 cups flour
½ teaspoon salt
6 1.6-ounce milk chocolate bars
⅔ cup chopped, toasted almonds

Cream together butter, brown sugar, egg yolk and vanilla. Stir in flour and salt.

❦ Pat mixture into 13″ × 10″ rectangle on greased cookie sheet with sides. Bake at 350 degrees until pale brown on top, approximately 20 to 25 minutes.

❦ Remove from oven and immediately place chocolate bars on top. Allow to melt, then spread evenly over shortbread. Sprinkle with nuts. Trim edges and cut into squares while still warm.

Floating Island
with Raspberry Sauce

LIGHT AS A CLOUD

Serves 4

Mold:

5 egg whites, at room temperature (use extra large eggs)
½ cup sugar
½ teaspoon vanilla

Sauce:

1 10-ounce package frozen raspberries
1 teaspoon kirsch

In metal bowl, beat egg whites until stiff. Add sugar and beat 20 seconds. Beat in vanilla. Pour into greased 1-quart mold, removing air bubbles with spatula. Place buttered parchment paper on top to prevent browning. Put mold in baking pan and add enough hot water to immerse mold halfway.

❦ Bake at 300 degrees for 20 minutes.

❦ Unmold onto platter, pouring off extra juices. Spoon sauce around mold and serve immediately.

❦ To make sauce, purée raspberries in food processor or blender. Strain to remove seeds. Stir in kirsch.

Cheesecake Bars

A CRUNCHY CRUST ADDS A UNIQUE
TEXTURE

Yields approximately 3 dozen

1 cup flour
¼ cup light brown sugar
1 cup finely chopped pecans
½ cup butter, melted
16 ounces cream cheese, softened
1⅓ cups sugar
2 teaspoons vanilla
2 eggs
2 cups sour cream

Mix flour, brown sugar, pecans and butter. Press into bottom of greased 9″ × 13″ baking pan. Bake at 350 degrees until light brown, approximately 10 to 15 minutes.

❦ Blend together cream cheese, 1 cup sugar and 1 teaspoon vanilla. Add eggs and beat well. Spread over crust and bake 20 minutes.

❦ Combine sour cream with remaining ⅓ cup sugar and 1 teaspoon vanilla. Pour over filling and bake 3 to 5 minutes. Cool and refrigerate before cutting.

Almond Tortoni

A NEAPOLITAN FROZEN DESSERT

Serves 12

1½ cups heavy cream
½   cup powdered sugar
1¼ cups macaroon crumbs
2   tablespoons dark rum, sherry, Kahlua or Irish cream liqueur
¼   cup chopped toasted almonds, plus extra for garnish
1   teaspoon vanilla

Beat cream and sugar until stiff peaks form.

❧ Set aside 3 tablespoons macaroon crumbs. Add remaining crumbs to mixture. Fold in liqueur, almonds and vanilla.

❧ Spoon tortoni into individual dishes or cupcake tins with paper liners. Sprinkle tops with reserved macaroon crumbs. Freeze until firm, at least 4 hours.

❧ Remove from freezer 10 minutes before serving. Garnish with chopped toasted almonds.

Raspberry Bread Pudding

FROM DESIGN CUISINE CATERERS

Serves 10

3   pints fresh raspberries
¼   cup sugar
2   tablespoons framboise
2   pounds brioche, crust removed
2   quarts Anglaise Sauce (see page 150)
2   peaches, skinned and sliced, for garnish
    Fresh mint for garnish

Marinate 2 pints raspberries with sugar for 2 hours. Purée raspberries, strain juice and reserve. Combine juice and framboise.

❧ Cut brioche into ½″ slices. Soak slices briefly in juice mixture. Line bottom and sides of 10-cup deep casserole with soaked brioche. Layer Anglaise Sauce, puréed raspberries and brioche slices 3 times to fill the mold, ending with brioche. Refrigerate overnight.

❧ Unmold onto serving plate. Pour remaining Anglaise Sauce and puréed raspberries over the top to form a design. Garnish with remaining pint of raspberries, peaches and mint.

Brown Betty Pudding

WONDERFUL HOMEY TASTE

Serves 6

1½ cups brown sugar
2   cups hot water
2   tablespoons butter
1   tablespoon cinnamon
1   cup flour
2   tablespoons baking powder
½   cup milk
½   cup raisins
½   cup chopped walnuts

In saucepan, combine 1 cup brown sugar, hot water and 1 tablespoon butter. Boil together 10 minutes to form a syrup. Pour into ovenproof dish.

❧ Combine remaining ½ cup brown sugar and 1 tablespoon butter. Stir in remaining ingredients. Spoon flour mixture into center of syrup. Do not stir.

❧ Bake at 400 degrees for 25 minutes. Serve warm with vanilla ice cream.

Louisiana Bread Pudding with Whiskey Sauce

INTOXICATING

Serves 10

½	cup butter
1	cup sugar
1½	cups water
3	eggs, beaten
1	13-ounce can evaporated milk
1	teaspoon vanilla
1	cup raisins
1	loaf French bread, broken into small pieces
½	teaspoon cinnamon

Whiskey Sauce:

½	cup butter
1	cup sugar
1	egg, beaten
¼–½	cup whiskey

Melt butter in saucepan. Add sugar and stir until dissolved. Add water and heat through, but do not boil. Whisk in eggs, evaporated milk and vanilla. Stir in raisins.

❧ Grease 9″ × 12″ casserole dish. Add bread. Pour mixture over bread. Sprinkle with cinnamon. Bake at 350 degrees for 45 minutes. Do not overbake.

❧ For whiskey sauce, slowly cook butter and sugar until sugar dissolves. Mixture should be thick and very hot. Add egg and beat quickly. Cool slightly and add whiskey. Serve hot or cold over bread pudding.

Vermont Apple Cobbler

SPLASHED WITH MAPLE SYRUP

Serves 6–8

6–8	large tart apples, peeled and sliced
½	cup sugar
¾	cup gingersnap crumbs
1	tablespoon flour
1	teaspoon cinnamon
¼	teaspoon salt
½	cup coarsely chopped walnuts or pecans
¼	cup butter, melted
⅓	cup maple syrup

Arrange half the apple slices in buttered baking dish. Combine sugar, gingersnap crumbs, flour, cinnamon, salt, nuts and butter. Spread half of mixture over apples. Layer with remaining apples and top with remaining crumb mixture. Bake at 350 degrees for 45 minutes.

❧ Heat maple syrup to boiling point and pour over cobbler. Bake an additional 15 minutes.

Pear Tarte Tatin

CARAMELIZED TOPPING COMPLEMENTS THE PEAR PASTRY

Serves 8

2	tablespoons unsalted butter
½	cup sugar
4	large Bosc pears, ripe but firm
1	tablespoon Armagnac or brandy
1	sheet frozen puff pastry, rolled into 10″ circle
	Vanilla ice cream or sweetened whipped cream

Melt butter in 9″ iron pan over medium-high heat. Add sugar, stirring constantly. Cook until mixture turns golden. Remove from heat.

❧ Peel and halve pears, removing cores. Toss pears gently with Armagnac or brandy, then place in caramel with round sides down and narrow ends towards center.

❧ Cut 5 1″ slits around center of thawed pastry and lay on top of fruit, molding to contours of pears. Set pan in 400 degree oven and bake for 30 minutes or until pears are tender and crust is browned. Remove from oven and let stand 1 minute. Invert serving plate on top of pan and flip over quickly. Spoon any remaining caramel over pears immediately. Serve with ice cream or sweetened whipped cream.

Blankenberry Cream

A LUXURIOUS TOPPING
FOR SUMMER FRUITS

Serves 6–8

4   egg yolks
1   cup sugar
6   tablespoons brandy or Cointreau
2   cups heavy cream

Beat egg yolks until pale and thick. Gradually beat in sugar, then brandy.

❧ In separate bowl, beat cream until soft peaks form. Fold cream into egg mixture. Chill at least 3 hours or overnight to set. Spoon over fresh fruit.

Gratin of Raspberries and Passion Fruit with Gingered Tuiles

FROM CHEF DOUGLAS MCNEILL,
THE FOUR SEASONS HOTEL

Serves 6

1¼   pounds raspberries
4   passion fruit
5   egg yolks
1   tablespoon water
2   tablespoons raspberry liqueur
3   tablespoons sugar
1½   tablespoons heavy cream

Divide raspberries among 6 individual dishes. Remove all pulp from passion fruit and pass through sieve. Combine pulp with egg yolks and water. Add 1 tablespoon liqueur and 2 tablespoons sugar.

❧ Set in double boiler over low heat and whisk until slightly thickened, about 3 to 4 minutes. Remove from heat and add cream and remaining liqueur.

❧ Spoon sauce over berries and sprinkle with remaining 1 tablespoon sugar. Place under broiler until golden brown. Serve with gingered tuiles.

Gingered Tuiles:

Yields 30

6   tablespoons butter, softened
½   cup light brown sugar
¼   cup light corn syrup
½   cup ground almonds
½   cup flour
    Pinch of salt
½   teaspoon ground ginger
1   teaspoon finely chopped crystallized ginger

Combine all ingredients until smooth. Let stand for 1 hour.

❧ Drop dough by rounded teaspoonfuls onto greased baking sheet. Using fork, spread mixture to 2½″ to 3″ circles. Bake at 375 degrees for 6 to 7 minutes or until golden brown. Remove from oven.

❧ When cool enough to handle, remove cookies with a spatula and place on rolling pin until cooled. (Be extremely careful as cookies are fragile.) Can be stored in an airtight container for 3 to 4 days.

COOKBOOK COMMITTEE

Chairman
Elizabeth Roberts

Design
Angela Desmond Bowe

Editorial
Jody Dove

Final Recipe Testing
Carol Williams Kelley

Marketing
Beverley McClinton

Final Testers

Karen Atkinson
Katherine Cheek
Grayson Harris
Jennifer Kemp
Jean Krafft
Laura Lawler
Susan MacDonald
Colby Manly
Karen Metz
Mary Ann Reed
Joyce Rollow
Alexandra Woodson
Andrea Young

Editors

Karen Brown
Carolyn Grant-Suttie
Linda Newbern
Susan Pyle
Cynthia Shade
Virginia Shields
Cynthia vanden Beemt

Design

Elizabeth Durrie
Elizabeth Hart
Nancy Kiechel
Barbara Lamade
Patricia Lammers
Margaret Tilghman

Marketing

Cheryl Alford
Elizabeth Bailey
Lizette Corro-Nobil
Darby Gingery
Susan Guillory
Darlene Harmon
Catherine Martens
Elizabeth Nibley
Nancy Piper
Paula Sigg
Ellie Wright

Chapter Chairmen

Linda Couch
Carol Kelley
Laura Lawler
Susan MacDonald
Colby Manly
Lynn Russell
Baldwin Tillman

ACKNOWLEDGMENTS

Photography props contributed by:

The Brass Knob
Washington, D.C.

Dumbarton House,
NSCDA
Washington, D.C.

Offices of the Secretary of
the Navy and the Chief
of Naval Operations
Washington, D.C.

Garfinckel's
Washington, D.C.

La Selection
Bethesda, Maryland

Little Caledonia
Washington, D.C.

Rooms and Gardens
Washington, D.C.

Vignettes
Bethesda, Maryland

Mr. Jay C. Banning
Washington, D.C.

Mrs. Richard E. Bowe
Arnold, Maryland

Mrs. Clarence Cottman
Alexandria, Virginia

Mr. & Mrs. C. Douglas
Elliott
Chevy Chase, Maryland

Ms. Katherine Fries
Alexandria, Virginia

Mrs. Leamon Holliman
Alexandria, Virginia

Mr. & Mrs. James Gill
Mersereau
Chevy Chase, Maryland

Mrs. William G. Roberts
Charlottesville, Virginia

**The Cookbook
Committee would like to
thank our many sister
Leagues who shared with
us their insights and
experiences.**

Recipes submitted by:

Julie A'Hearn
Cathy Alfandre
Demetra Economos Anas
Susan A. Andrews
Mrs. Gary J. Ansley
Kathi H. Antonio
Kim Armour
Karen E. Atkinson
Elizabeth Stewart Bailey
Boots Baldini
Mrs. John Ballantyne
Patricia Bancroft
Susana Baranano
Ann Barber
Brenda Barrett
Mimi Barringer
Jeffrey W. Bartlett
Melinda Baskin
Mrs. Charles Tucker Battle
Rebecca Beach
Susan Wadsworth Becks
Karen Belfield
Greta Benedict
Leslie D. Benson
Becky L. Bentson
Polly C. Best
Virginia H. Biddle
Sandi Birdsong
Emily C. Bish
Olivia Bissell
Peggy Bitsas
Heidi T. Bogardus
Leanne M. Boland
Mary Claire Bond
Alice B. Borrelli
Harriett Bosiack
Page Hart Boteler
Angela Desmond Bowe
Karen Bowles
Elizabeth Bowling
Ann K. Bowman
Margaret Boyd
Nancy Coleman Braddock
Elizabeth Bradfield
Marina Utgoff Braswell
Carol Brauninger
Lindsay Brice
Deborah Briggs
Susan Bright
Carol Brill
Joan Bertrand Brooks
Peggy Brooks
Karen Brown
Lynne M. Brown
Madeleine M. Brown
Graeme Browning
Marilyn Buchanan
Mimi Buchanan

Barbara Buchman
Elizabeth D. Buehler
Maura Fitzgerald Burke
Susan Burke
Susan L. Burns
Beulah Burrus
Barbara L. Bush
Jane Butler
Virgina Buxton
Molly Byock
Lisa Cabot
Virginia Camden
Karen H. Cameron
Mrs. Charles Camp
Mrs. John C. Camp
Lucie Ling Campbell
Karin M. Campion
Esther A. Capasse
Patricia J. Carlan
Barbara Carroll
Dorothy Carroll
Mary Beth Carroll
Mrs. Edward Cassidy, Jr.
Ann P. Casso
Cathy Cave
Susan Chadick
Virginia Chancey
Ellen Chaney
Jerry Chapman
Mrs. David Cheek
Mrs. George David Cheek
Barbara F. Cherry
Virginia M. Child
Carrie Clark
Jane Rath Clark
Peggy Clarke
Lydie Clay
Tina Cleland
Sharon Smithey Coale
Margaret E. Coloney
Sally Comiskey
Cynthia Conroy
Nancy Anne Cook
Lizette Corro-Nobil
Betty Wallace Corty
Linda Couch
Katherine Coudriet
Saralee Cowles
Judy Cox
Diana Crandall
Cathy Crawford
Mary Grace Crosby
Mrs. Greig Cummings, Jr.
Carole Currin
Janice Curtin
Mrs. Charles A. Cushman
Lois Czapiewski
Betsy McNeal Darling
Mary C. Denger
Brenda Destro

Mrs. Robert L. Dibbler
Susan Gardner Dickens
Suzzi Dickson
Rosemary Dircks
Marilyn Dorin
Katy Douglas
Mrs. Edward S. Dove III
Carole W. Drewyer
Jeannette V. Dubin
Jennifer J. Duckett
Elizabeth Durrie
Tanya Matthews Edmond
Alice R. Ellington
Carolyn A. Elliot
Lee Sawyer Elliott
J.W. Ellis
Mrs. Craig A. Etter
Eileen Evans
Susan Ewald
Barbara Cook Fabiani
Judy Fantle
Patricia Granfield Finan
Vicki Huff Fisk
Jeremy Fitzgerald
Sally Howell Fitzpatrick
Lizzie Flanagin
Becky Fleck
Bridget Flint
Anne Flues
Jennie Fogarty
Margot Foster
Nancy E. Foster
Judith W. Frank
Cynthia Z. Franklin
Danielle French
Diane Baldwin French
Alice Anne Freund
Ann E. Frogale
Bridget Funt
Anne T. Gaillard
Barbara Gahagan
Kim Gallagher
Mrs. Rhett W. Gano
George D. Garrett
Sarah Garrett
Mary Elizabeth Garver
Wendy Gasch
Elizabeth Gibney
Mrs. Julian E. Gillespie, Jr.
Suzanne Giordano
Jean Gloff
Mary Kirk Goehring
May Gold
Mary Goldberg
Peggy S. Graeter
Carolyn F. Grant-Suttie
Margie Deane Gray
Ellen M. Granum
Faith P. Greeley
India Gregory

Robbie Griffin
Mrs. Arthur L. Guillory
Eileen P. Gunzelman
Mrs. Lawrence Gustafson
Kathleen A. Halayko
Henry Haller
Saniya Hamady
Darlene Harmon
Constance Harriman
Cindy Harrington
Grayson L. Harris
Leslie Harrison
Elizabeth H. Hart
Lisa G. Hathaway
Martha Hawkins
Alice Heires
Gail MacLean Helmkamp
Adrienne Hensley
Nancy B. Heston
Barbara T. Higgins
Genevra Higginson
Shannon H. Hobbs
Katharine Hoehn
Suzanne Horntaker
Debbie Howard
Ann Morton Hubliston
Elizabeth Young Huckaby
Molly Huffman
Margery Huge
Muriel Poston Hughes
Susan V. Hussar
Dial Jackson
Jean Appleby Jackson
Amy Matthews Jacobs
Laura W. Jacobs
Regina Jahr
Mrs. F. Winston James
Anne C. Johns
Karen A. Johnson
Margo M. Johnson
JoAnne Holladay Johnston
Debbie Jones
George K. Jones
Idalina M. Jones
Nancy Kachline
Patricia Katkish
Trish Katz
Carol Kelley
Jennifer Kemp
Jane Kendrick
Melinda M. Kenney
Elizabeth Youmans Kepley
Martha Kendrick Kettmer
Mrs. Brian S. Kidney
Nancy Savage Kiechel
Melissa P. Killmer
Ruth Anne King
Cheryl Kinney
Elizabeth Kinney
Carol A. Kinzer

Winnie Kinzer
Priscilla Keller Kirby
Lynn S. Klein
Missy Klineman
Mary Ann Knapp
Susan Koehler
Rebecca Kojm
Jean W. Krafft
Mrs. Charles Kurtz, Jr.
Phoebe B. Kurz
Karen Kuzemka
Barbara S. Lamade
Sue N. Landa
P. Kim Landford
Theresa B. Lange
Linda K. Larson
Mrs. Jonathan H. Lasley
Martha Lechner
Joan-Marie Presley Lintvet
Carol A. Lively
Mrs. Henry Malcolm Lloyd
Sharon H. Longabaugh
Beatrice Locher
Bea Loos
Patsy Lynch
Susan H. MacDonald
Sanford J. McAllister
Ashley McArthur
Beverley B. McClinton
Gina McClinton
Virginia McKaig
Jill McKee
Rebecca S. McMahan
Janet McNamara
Emily McNaughton
Eve Macintyre
Marnie Mack
Terri Maes
Anne Mahoney
Lyn Maness
Colby Chapman Manly
Cathy Martens
Lynn Martenstein
Deborah Martin
Vicki Martyak
Mrs. William Mason
Kim Massengill
Beverly A. Massey
Karen Mathis
Linda Mattingly
Lacy M. Matzner
Gayle Elizabeth Maurin
Pamela R. Mefford
Kathleen D. Merchant
Helen W. Metcalf
Karen McCleary Metz
Margaret L. Mickler
Elizabeth S. Middleton
Erin Davies Miller
Martha L. Miller

Andrea Gene Mitts
Margaret Todd Monrose
Jane D. Mooney
Janet Abney Moore
Molly Moore
Catherine Moran
Mrs. Robert H. Moran, Jr.
Penny C. Morrill
Ellen F. Morrison
Mrs. Stanley Mortensen
Mary Jane C. Mortimer
Mary Beth Mueller
Barbara Mullarkey
Mary C. Mulligan
Susan T. Mundy
Debbie Murphy
Libby Murphy
Donna D. Naybor
Mrs. William E. Naylor, Jr.
Sharon L. Nemeroff
Jane Nettles
Linda Baird Newbern
Liz Nibley
Jennifer Nichols
Barbara Nixon
Mariana Nork
Frances Norris
Lisa Nouss
Alice Diggs Nulsen
Mrs. Patrick O'Donnell
L. Susan Ogletree-Conner
Jane Ramsay Olmsted
Suzanne Higgins O'Malley
Wendy O'Meara
Kathy Galiher Ott
Lisa Ourisman
Susan Pantzer
Ginny Parsley
Elizabeth Paulson
Karen Greeley Pena
Brooke Perry
Sarah English Perry
Nancy Pevrelli
Mary Phelps
Ann Pierce
Ann S. Piesli
Nancy Piper
Marie Chapin Plumley
Julie Pohl
Babette Prevot
Mary Ann Prevot
Elizabeth Pryor
Mrs. Fay Purdin
Susan Clinard Pyle
Peter Raffalski
Mary Ann Reed
Amy Harvey Reese
Debra Ann Repeta
Brooke Reuther
Sara Kate Rex

Alison G. Rice
Charlotte Rich
Murray Richey
Ann Riser
Elizabeth Haley Roberts
Lauren Robinson
Beth Rocks
Anne Rogers
Rebecca B. Rogers
Sarah Rogers
Joyce Rollow
Catherine Brown Rose
Mary Jane Rosenbaum
Marta Miller Ross
Mrs. Randolph Royen
Lynn Rudolf
Lynn Pearson Russell
A. Leslie St. Louis
Lorraine L. Salisbury
Brooks Saltsman
Martha Lee Sanders
Patricia Savage
Patricia P. Schieffer
Deborah A. Schneider
Lynn Schoolfield
Marilyn Seely
Judy Seibels
Medina Semb
Kathy Boykin Semmes
Cheryl W. Sensenbrenner
Sally Seward
Mrs. Edna S. Sewell
Cynthia S. Shade
Jody Shaner
Virginia B. Shields
Anne H. Simms
Elizabeth Simms
Cora Simpson
Susan D. Simpson
Catherine S. Singleton
Dinny Sisley
Mary Lynn Skutky
Cindy Ann Smet
Kathleen O'Connell Smet
Carrie C. Smith
Charlotte A. Smith
Marian Kaiser Smith
Virginia H. Smith
Mrs. William C. Smith
Deborah Snowhite-Kutner
Ann Spitler
Carol H. Stackhouse
Ellen Stark
Mrs. Sam Stein
Cynthia J. Steuart
Mrs. Guy T. Stewart III
Elfi Stitz
Ann S. Stock
Mary Kiernan Storz
Roxanne Stosur

Patty Strohm
Holly Hyneik Sukenik
Lynn B. Summerlin
Anne Taylor
Christopher A. Taylor
Bettie Thompson
Beth Tiernan
Pamela M. Tiernan
Baldwin Tillman
Gail Turner
Cindy vanden Beemt
Connie Cook Vanderpool
Mrs. T. A. Vanderver, Jr.
Ann Morris Van Kirk
Marilyn Wilson Van Story
Marilyn Varela
Mary Claire Veith
Mrs. John Vesely
Mrs. John F. Wall
Joni Wallace
Elizabeth A. Watts
Leanne P. Weber
Cynthia Caldwell Weglicki
Robin K. Weiss
Charlotte M. Weller
Karen F. Wells
Ann Paine West
Mary T. Wheeler
Lynn Whipple
Barbara B. White
Mary S. White
Elizabeth H. Wildhack
Cynthia L. Williams
Holly Williams
Joyce L. Williams
Mrs. Harter Williams
Catherine Wilson
Heather N. Willson
Maio Winkler
Emmy Woehrle
Patricia J. Wohl
Jean D. Wolf
Cameron Woods
Mrs. Walter Woodson
Kay W. Woodward
Wendy Woodward
Eleanor G. Wright
Andrea T. Young
Mary Clarke Zigo
Diane Zutant

INDEX

28 DAYS

DATE DUE			
MAR 2 3 '98			
APR 2 0 '98			
SEP 1 6 2011			